BRUSHES WITH THE GREATS

THE STORY OF A FOOTBALLER/CRICKETER

By Kevin Smallbone

BASED ON THE SPORTING LIFE OF BERNARD HARRISON

ACKNOWLEDGEMENTS

Thanks above all to Bernard for all the hours spent plumbing his memories and for access to his memorabilia and statistics, to Rod Bransgrove for his personal view, to Gerald Williams and Tony Baker for their forewords, and to Alan Mackrill for his help. Also thanks are due to all those who assisted by giving their thoughts and reminiscences, including Clive Harrison, Ian Crossley, Terry Long, Roy Woodcock, Bryan Timms, Peter Haslop, Alan Castell, Malcolm Heath, Tom Allcock, Ian Henderson of the *Hampshire Chronicle,* Tony Godfrey, Admiral Sir Brian Brown, David Gahan, Philip Watts and others.

Published by *Sportingmemoriesonline.com*

Printed by Greenhouse Graphics

ISBN 0-9537880-2-4

BY THE SAME AUTHOR

Farewell to May's Bounty
HAMPSHIRE COUNTY CRICKET
At Basingstoke 1906-2000
ISBN 0-9537880-1-6
Hardback 120pp
£12.95

The Story of the
Basingstoke Derby Match
Basingstoke Town
v.
Thornycroft Athletic
1900-1972
ISBN 0-9537880-0-8
Paperback £5.99

CONTENTS

A PERSONAL VIEW
From Rod Bransgrove,
Chairman Hampshire CCC

My daughter, Lucy, was barely seven years old when we were enjoying a short family holiday on the Channel Island of Guernsey.

Bernard Harrison, whom I have always known as Bernie, was also holidaying on the island and we had arranged to meet one evening for a drink or two. Bernie taught maths at Farleigh School, near Andover, and was alarmed to hear that Lucy was struggling with arithmetic in his school's pre-prep. He exchanged a few amusing mathematical anecdotes with her triggering an interest in numbers which simply had not been present before.

Lucy is now approaching her teens; she excels in mathematics and has retained an enjoyment of the subject to this day.

I offer this story merely to dispel the theory that a Jack of all trades can be master of none. Bernie Harrison has proved the exception to this rule.

Whether as a cricketer, a footballer, a coach of either of the above sports and others or a teacher of mathematics, Bernie has never been prepared to accept mediocrity as his benchmark. He doesn't like it much in others but will not tolerate it in himself. This is what sets him apart from other people.

It is widely acknowledged that he was unlucky not to have played more 1st class cricket than he did but Hampshire featured the awesome combination of Roy Marshall, Jimmy Gray and Henry Horton at the time and this, coupled with his professional football commitments towards the end of each season, contrived to restrict his opportunities.

Nevertheless, he was one of the last of very few players to have featured at the top domestic levels of both football and cricket. That phenomenal record of playing for his beloved Basingstoke Cricket Club in seven separate decades further testifies to his extraordinary skill and longevity.

So this Jack truly is the Master of all his trades; the only one I have ever met. It is also said by some that Bernie could talk for England - if only someone would listen! Well, I for one will always listen because there is infinite wisdom in his words. In fact this is how we first met in the mid

1980s at the bar of our local squash club. Having been introduced by another cricket enthusiast, we engaged in a dialogue that took us well into the wee small hours and encompassed a good few brandies. It is a dialogue which I am happy to say has continued intermittently for over fifteen years and one that I hope will be sustained for a long time to come.

FOOTBALL FOREWORD
By Gerald Williams, Sky Sports

When Bernard Harrison, like a will o' the wisp, was dazzling on the right wing for Crystal Palace, I was the local sports editor on The Croydon Advertiser. As such, I used to cover most of their matches and got to know the players well.

Two things made Bernard stand out. First was his skill in dribbling at high speed: it was exceptional. Second was the lad himself. It was not merely his unusual talent at two major professional sports, but his genuine love of sport.

Not every sporting star I have met through the years - in fact, few - have possessed this enduring care for the way his sport is played, as well as for the people in it. Too many come into the professional game with an attitude of giving it 'their best shot' then moving on into another lifestyle with little thought subsequently for the game that originally set them up.

Bernard was always a thinker, always probing to find out more. And his concern was not merely for himself but for the game and its people.

I am fascinated by the element of chance in our lives. For example, would a Danish tennis player have gone on to become chief executive of Smith Kline Beecham if he hadn't had a dreadful line call at Wimbledon one year that possibly cost him a place in the semi-finals of the singles. I once asked Jan Leschley that, and we chuckled together.

Similarly, if the young son of a Cardiff spaghetti restaurateur hadn't been told by the manager of Swansea City that he wouldn't make the grade at the Vetch Field, would he have tried his luck in Italy and ended up an Italian international striker who later played for New York Cosmos, had an executive job at Warner Bros Communications and later owned Lazio? I asked Giorgio Chinaglia that in his plush Manhattan office one day, and we wondered together about chance.

I ponder how chance affected Bernard Harrison's footballing career. When he was dazzling, and all the scouts were turning up, where might his career have gone if Cyril Spiers had let him go? We'll never know.

But as I head for retirement, and I remember with real affection the footballers and tennis players who had something extra about them, something in their spirit, I suppose, Bernard Harrison is one I especially enjoy remembering.

CRICKET FOREWORD
By Tony Baker, Chief Executive
Hampshire CCC

To be asked to write a foreword for this book is a real honour. Bernard Harrison knows and is known by so many people in the sporting fraternity of Hampshire and beyond and it is difficult to understand why I was asked to contribute in this way. The thought that there had been an enormous number of rejections only briefly passed through my brain.

Along with many local football supporters, I remember Bernard playing for the Saints a few times. Otherwise I can't contribute any worthwhile comments on the football side of this story.

As far as cricket is concerned, however, our paths have crossed regularly for forty years or more, although I can only recall playing in the same side with Bernard on one occasion- for Hampshire 2nd XI against Gloucestershire 2nd XI at Dean Park in 1959 (or was it 1960?) when we opened the bowling together. No doubt Bernard can provide the details, if asked, through his mine of statistical information.

All of my Club Cricket was played for Old Tauntonians (on Saturdays) and the Southampton Touring Club (on Sundays). It was my great fortune that the latter always played an all-day match against Basingstoke and North Hants CC at Mays Bounty on Whit Monday and that the O.T.'s did the same on August Bank Holiday Monday. I know one's memory plays tricks but so many of these games produced great cricket and wonderful incidences. The teams got to know each other so well that these matches were almost like family re-unions (but much more enjoyable!).

On the field, there was an awful lot of chat - humorous mainly and certainly never malicious. Bernard was always at the centre of it particularly if there was a hint of a delayed declaration by either side. Off the field, the fact that both Southampton Clubs contained players who had been professionals at cricket and football alongside Bernard produced so many yarns (unrepeatable in this book!). Invariably the bar rocked with laughter for ages before we reluctantly left for Southampton already looking to the next meeting. They were wonderful days!

Although there was a certain amount of 'mickey taking', we always looked forward to Bernard's up-date on the number of great cricketers that were coming through the ranks at Basingstoke or indeed at Farleigh

School. He certainly was a great believer in the youngsters that he coached in all sports even if they turned out to be mere mortals eventually.

Bernard undoubtedly has a real talent for coaching and a great rapport with young sportsmen. There must literally be thousands who have derived enormous benefit from his expertise and enthusiasm - they have been extremely fortunate.

I feel sure that this book will be a great interest to many local sportsmen who have known and admired Bernard over the years. Hopefully we will be able to enjoy his company for many years to come.

INTRODUCTION

A 'Nearly Man'

Bernard Harrison is one of the last of a very special but now extinct breed - the footballer/cricketers who had the talent and opportunity to play both professional soccer and first-class cricket.

The playing seasons of the two premier national sports nowadays overlap to such an extent that a playing career encompassing both is now impossible, particularly given the training and fitness levels required, the intensity of competition and the contractual issues which make specialisation essential. Phil Neville, the Manchester United and England footballer, was a very promising young cricketer - captaining England at under 15 level - but he was forced to choose between the two sports even before he left school.

Even in the late 1950s and early 1960s when Bernard played cricket for Hampshire and soccer for Crystal Palace, Southampton and Exeter City he was a member of a threatened species as it was only possible to play both games successfully if the respective clubs were very cooperative. Inevitably the career in one or both games suffered.

In the great days of amateur sport before the First World War it was more common for exceptionally talented players to reach the top in more than one sport, notably of course C. B. Fry, who was probably the greatest ever all-round sportsman. Among his other athletic achievements, he played full-back for Southampton in the FA Cup Final of 1902 and won an international soccer cap as well as being one of the leading batsmen of his generation and captaining the England cricket team. As professionals came to dominate both soccer and cricket, however, specialisation became inevitable and by the early 1950s it was mainly the amateurs from Oxbridge who kept the Corinthian spirit alive. Players like Douglas Insole, Peter May, and Donald Carr all went on to play cricket for England, but had also captained their teams in the Varsity soccer matches played at White Hart Lane in the early 1950s. Indeed both Insole and Carr also played in the FA Amateur Cup Final, at that time still a leading event in the sporting calendar.

In professional sport, too, there remained exceptions. Both of the Middlesex twins Denis Compton and Bill Edrich also played top class football, the former as outside-left for Arsenal - winning an FA Cup winners medal in 1950 - and for England in wartime and Victory internationals, and the latter for Spurs in the late 1930s. But Denis

Compton's experience also served as a warning of the risks involved because his cricket career was significantly foreshortened by a knee injury picked up on the soccer field. Denis' brother Leslie, the Middlesex wicket-keeper, himself won an FA Cup winners' medal with Arsenal as well as two full England caps as a centre-half.

Remarkably, Willie Watson and Arthur Milton extended the sobriquet 'Double International' into the 1950s. Watson played in 23 Tests for England and also won four soccer caps as a wing-half during a career with Huddersfield Town, Sunderland, and Halifax Town. Milton made 75 appearances at outside-right for Arsenal, winning one England cap, and was a Gloucestershire batsman who played for England on the ill-fated tour of Australia in 1958-59. He kept his football career short, however, and extended his cricket playing days into his forties.

Other cricketers flirted with a soccer career — such as Brian Close who, as well as being something of a young prodigy as a cricketer, played football for England Youth and was first on Leeds United's books, then Arsenal's, and finally Bradford City's, but only in the end made six first team appearances for Bradford. Similarly Ken Suttle, a good left-hand batsman and slow left-arm bowler for Sussex in the fifties and sixties, was in his younger days a promising footballer with Chelsea and Brighton and Hove Albion, for whom he made just three league appearances.

Jack Dyson of Lancashire and Manchester City succeeded for a short period at combining both disciplines - making 150 County Championship appearances and 63 in the Football League as an inside-forward, scoring the winning goal in the FA Cup Final of 1956. Another cricketer who won an FA Cup winners' medal was Jim Standen who was West Ham's goalkeeper eight years later. He combined a good football career with his county cricket as a pace bowler with Worcestershire in the sixties. Another goalkeeper/cricketer in the sixties and seventies was Jim Cumbes who was with Tranmere Rovers and then WBA and Aston Villa while also bowling fast-medium, again mainly for Worcestershire.

The two most successful of the latter-day footballer/cricketers were both Yorkshiremen, Chris Balderstone and Ken Taylor. Both played as batsmen in a handful of Tests for England without really having the career figures to justify it, Taylor over the 1959-64 period and Balderstone as late as 1976 while with Leicestershire. As a footballer Balderstone is best remembered for his time with Carlisle United (369 games with 68 goals from inside-forward) but he lost the captaincy because of his commitment to cricket. Taylor was a centre-half with Huddersfield Town and Bradford Park Albion over a period of thirteen years up to 1966.

Worthy of mention too is Graham Cross, who gave priority to his football career and won an under-23 cap and made nearly 500 appearances for Leicester City (1960-75) as a defender, but who was also a useful all-round cricketer for Leicestershire. Also in the fifties and sixties the South African Stuart Leary successfully combined professional careers in both sports, football as a centre-forward mainly for Charlton Athletic and cricket as a middle order batsman for Kent. A familiar figure, too, at this time on the London county cricket and football scene was Ron Tindall. He was a good-looking right hand batsman and occasional off break bowler and, for most of his football career, a centre-forward. He had a very promising beginning in both games - joining the dominant county cricket side of the fifties, Surrey, in 1956 while making 160 appearances and scoring 67 goals for Chelsea alongside Jimmy Greaves. Things tailed off a little thereafter. He remained with Surrey for ten years and had several football clubs, finishing his career as a defender with Portsmouth (1964-69).

Phil Neale, a member of the England cricket management team in recent years, managed to combine careers right into the mid-80s - as a middle order batsman for Worcestershire and midfield player for Lincoln City. But it led him into conflict with the clubs and on one occasion he was suspended by Lincoln for his loyalty to cricket. He and the other talented all-rounders before him were very much the exception, flying in the face of received wisdom: the compelling need for professional sportsmen to concentrate on one sport. Even Ian Botham ignored this reality for a while, risking injury while making a few appearances for Doncaster Rovers.

Bernard Harrison as an aspiring professional footballer/cricketer back in the fifties, then, was seeking to join a very exclusive club. He was also swimming against the tide of history. Even then it had become a very difficult balancing act. A few Hampshire cricketers had managed to combine the two careers in the past, most notably Johnny Arnold who won single international caps in both football and cricket in the 1930s. Of the Hampshire playing staff when Bernard joined in 1957 Henry Horton had been a craggy wing-half for Blackburn and Southampton, while Mike Barnard was an inside-forward on Portsmouth s books. On reflection perhaps Bernard Harrison was too talented for his own good, had he specialised he would undoubtedly have progressed further in the game of his choice. Inevitably the distraction of one affected progress in the other.

His story is a fascinating one. Tales of batting with Roy Marshall or as a youngster facing Frank Tyson or competing against football legends such as Johnny Haynes and the young Duncan Edwards. Although restricted in his appearances he was with Hampshire CCC when the

County won its first championship in 1961 and with Southampton FC when they won promotion to the Second Division. He was feted as the new Stanley Matthews when with Crystal Palace. He seemed to have the world at his feet when he was the star of the Third Division South league representative side and was being pursued by top clubs. But within four years he was in non-league football.

So his story is also an indictment of English professional football at that time. An indictment of the management which was both insular and narrow-minded: of its suspicion of individuality, skill and flair (a suspicion which still endures today); of its vindictiveness towards intelligent players who dared to challenge the conventional wisdom of outmoded coaching methods; and of the retain and transfer system which still gave the clubs absolute control over players careers.

By common consent, too, he was one of the unluckiest of Hampshire cricketers. Once he became free of the diversion of league football at the end of the 1960/61 season, he wanted to concentrate on developing his cricket career. He had served a long apprenticeship and his consistent batting for the Second X1 seemed to demand a longer run of matches in the County Championship. An overture from Nottinghamshire was resisted by Hampshire who seemed to be grooming him for the next available first team slot. But when the club found that it had to reduce its playing staff at the end of the 1962 season the axe fell on Bernard.

So he was to remain a 'Nearly Man' destined never to realise his full potential in professional sport. Looking back, however, he would not have wanted to have compromised and to have missed his brushes with the greats and the experience of appearing in front of packed terraces at football grounds around the country or of coming down the steps at Lords to open the batting. And the early end of his involvement in professional sport was to catapult him into a career as teacher and coach which ultimately was to provide the most satisfying and rewarding phase of his professional life.

CHAPTER ONE

SCHOOLBOY STAR

Coronation Year

1953 was Coronation Year, the dawn of a new Elizabethan age, a defining year in Britain's recovery from the gloom of the post-war period. It was a great year of sporting achievement and this played a significant part in lifting the public mood. Public consciousness of sport was at an all-time high with increasing coverage of sporting events on radio and, increasingly, television. Stanley Matthews won his first FA Cup Final winners' medal in what became forever known as the 'Matthews Final' and Denis Compton hit the winning boundary to win a famous victory in the final Test against Australia and to regain the Ashes for the first time since 1932-33. In other sports Gordon Richards won the Coronation Derby and was knighted, Gordon Pirie was the athlete of the year, while Sterling Moss and Mike Hawthorn were two young British drivers beginning to make an impact in the world of international motor racing. Even Mount Everest was conquered. In amateur soccer Pegasus, the combined University Club of Oxford and Cambridge, thrilled a Wembley crowd of 100,000 with their superb flowing football in winning the F.A. Amateur Cup Final by six goals to nil.

But with hindsight it is possible to see that such confidence in English sporting achievement was perhaps misplaced. The year of 1953 also bequeathed another more significant landmark for its football. England's complacency about their leadership of the football world was shaken in November by the 6-3 defeat by the wonderfully skilled Hungarians at Wembley, the scale and manner of which was a serious challenge to English coaching methods. That the result pointed to a fundamental superiority in technique was further emphasised by the away defeat by 7-1 in Budapest six months later. An outcry in the national press resulted and the Football Association was moved to set up various technical committees to review English methods.

For some commentators too the increasingly professional approach to football and cricket was nurturing an unacceptably negative approach to both games. In cricket the England side - under its first professional captain, Len Hutton - had at times adopted 'go-slow' tactics in the Test series against Australia, tactics which were deplored by the purists who considered that the more adventurous team had lost. The County Championship also had become a rather turgid affair with an increasing proportion of matches ending in draws. Similarly there was criticism of the ultra defensive play which had come to characterise British football and of the training methods which to a large extent relied on 'lapping' and placed too little emphasis on the skills of the game. Although the days were long gone when the best amateur teams could compete on a par with professionals, the 'fifties saw the final flowering of amateur football in the national spotlight. The F.A. Amateur Cup Final could still command crowds of 100,000 at Wembley and the artistry of Pegasus' adventurous and constructive football was in stark contrast to much of that seen in the professional game.

In that year of great events in 1953 an aspiring young sportsman in Andover Hampshire, seemed to have the world at his feet. The story of Bernard Harrison's sporting feats as a schoolboy could have been plucked straight from the pages of *Boy's Own* - the hero of his House who was *Victor Ludorum* and captain of the school X1s at both association football and cricket, and who went on to represent Hampshire schools and England schools at both disciplines. Indeed his precocious excellence as an all-round sportsman - including athletics, tennis, badminton, hockey, fives - recalled something of the Corinthian ideal of sporting achievement. By 1953, his final year at school, he had won selection for the second year running for the England secondary schools representative sides at both cricket and soccer, opening the batting and the bowling as well as putting on dazzling displays as a goal-scoring winger. He had taken his first steps towards a professional career in sport, playing for Worcestershire Second X1 and signing amateur forms for Portsmouth FC, one of the leading sides of the day who had won successive First Division championships in 1948-49 and 1949-50.

Schooldays

But his very first term at school had been an unhappy one at St Johns in Worcester, although his talent had been recognised even at the age of five. He left there with a report which was brief but accurate: it merely read "exceptional at all games". Worcester was the home of the family on his mother Pearl's side and, as Bernard puts it, all the offspring "were sent there to be born". He was born there on 28th September 1934 and was christened Bernard Reginald Stanhope Harrison, with the three initials possibly conferred by dad with an eye to future cricket scorecards! Father Reg was a headmaster at Titchfield in Hampshire at the time and a cricket fanatic, a useful club cricketer and captain of Basingstoke & North Hants Cricket Club.

Bernard's earliest sporting recollections are of cricket contests with younger brother Clive (himself a future Hampshire amateur cricketer and also adorned with three initials - C.N.P.) played under an enormous weeping beech tree in the grounds of the family-run nurseries at Worcester where they spent their holidays. These involved 'inter-county' matches played with a tennis ball where the brothers had to adopt the bowling and batting styles of the heroes they sought to emulate - batting and bowling both right and left-handed as appropriate. His first visit to a first-class ground was also at Worcester during the war and left a compelling memory of the power and majesty of the incomparable Wally Hammond who scored a century for the RAF including a square drive for six and the biggest straight six Bernard has ever seen.

Bernard finally in 1939 settled into the village school in Hampshire, where his father had taken over as headmaster, at Preston Candover, a village some seven miles from Basingstoke. Living in the schoolhouse was somewhat stifling for a young boy since he was never truly free of school, while some of the children were a little wary of mixing with the son of a very strict headmaster. Most of his young friends in this farming community had broad rural accents - few had ever travelled beyond the village boundaries - and Bernard soon acquired the rounded Hampshire vowels, tempered to a sort of 'Hampshire/Cockney' when some evacuees arrived.

However his cricket developed rapidly under Dad's watchful eye and he had all the strokes by the time he was ten. Bernard and Clive played in the coal yard behind the school with stumps chalked onto a door, using a tennis ball with a cricket stump as the bat. Both Bernard at just eleven years of age and his friend John Harman aged thirteen from the school had trials for Hampshire Schools under 15s in 1946, but much to Dad's annoyance Bernard was relegated to 12th man for the match v. West Sussex because he was small even for his tender years. He also remembers his father showing him off at Basingstoke club matches, bowling to him in front of the pavilion notably on an occasion in 1945 before a fixture against the Buccaneers, a side which included some county players such as J.G. W. Davies of Kent and the writer E. M. Wellings.

Young Bernard at the crease -
nets at Peter Symonds 1947

And the same stroke some
forty years later

His parents thought he would develop more self-reliance if he attended a boarding school and in September 1946 Bernard went to Peter Symonds School in Winchester, previously a public school but by then a grammar school - subject to Local Education Authority control - which nevertheless very much retained its former ethos. This was a rude shock to an eleven year-old who had known such a sheltered upbringing and the first term was "absolute hell", particularly as he was the only new boy and therefore "fag" to every other boy in the house. His 'Hampshire-Cockney' accent caused amusement at school, but when he went home for half-term his mother was equally amused at his newly acquired posh tones.

At the end of his first term he had to be inaugurated into the house. This ritual involved having to drink a concoction made up of Andrews Liver Salts, vinegar and pepper with half an inch of mustard round the top of the glass, and then singing a song standing on a table, his being "Way down upon the Swanee River". Much to Bernard's disgust this practice was banned thereafter, so he was never able to get his own back.

School life improved vastly from there on and he thoroughly enjoyed it and was in the thick of any pranks such as raids on other dormitories. As a result he sometimes suffered at the hands of sadistic prefects who thought nothing of administering six of the best with a hockey stick or army belt. When he himself eventually became a Prefect he never hit another boy nor ever needed to.

On one occasion he even got his Maths teacher 'Harry' Hawkins into a scrape. Tom Allcock, an exact contemporary at the school, remembers that *"he persuaded 'Harry' to juggle (or attempt to) five tennis balls - having demonstrated how it should be done. 'Harry's vain attempt to copy him was interrupted by the Headmaster 'Doc' Freeman, leaving 'Harry' to concoct an unlikely tale about demonstrating some abstruse relationship concerning spheres in motion. Bernard was unrepentant."*

Bernard showed early evidence that he was to become the best all-round sportsman the school had ever had. Admiral Sir Brian Brown (Second Sea Lord, retired) recalls: *"Bernard and I joined Peter Symonds in September 1946. I was competent. He was a colossus who towered over the rest of us despite his slight build and stature. Faced with a ball or a shuttlecock he just excelled at every game – cricket, soccer, hockey, badminton, tennis, squash, and fives. As well as representing England schools at cricket and soccer, he was a badminton All England semi-finalist. He was a formidable sprinter, miler and cross-country runner. And he was a very accomplished chess player too! To compete against him in House matches was often chastening. To play with him was always comforting. We admired him, we respected him, and – because there was no side to him – we liked him".*

His only sporting predecessor of real note at the school was Dennis Martin who had been a half-back with Bournemouth in the late forties and early fifties. However a contemporary of Bernard's, Archie Warr, would have run him close had he not been handicapped with polio. As it was he excelled as a wicket-keeper, a goalkeeper in both football and hockey, and at badminton. As a batsman his timing was quite amazing - with his runs of necessity mostly acquired from boundaries. On one occasion he was to score 129 out of a total of 142 in an Old Boys' match. Bernard considers that he had great natural talent and that, but for his handicap, he would have achieved great things not least because of his determination. He is now a very successful surgeon in the U.S.A.

The Long and
the Short of it -openers
Lockyer and Harrison

At the age of twelve Bernard found himself in the Senior House cricket X1 (under 19s), opening the batting at all of four feet nothing with a partner who was 6 feet five! He also secured the place he had narrowly missed the year before in the Hampshire colts side and held it for three years. In his first game against West Sussex it was his bowling which prospered to take four wickets for eight runs, at a quickish pace but with a longer run than was justified (something he admits he never corrected). In his final year for the County colts he scored 65 at May's Bounty before being run out, opening with a certain Peter Sainsbury in a win also against West Sussex.

PETER SYMONDS SOCCER TEAM 1952
Back row-Hockey, May, Whatmore, Roberts, Allcock, Mr Smith
Front Row - NK, John Marshall, Witcher, 'Doc' Freeman, Oxborrow, Harrison, Stocker

PETER SYMONDS CRICKET TEAM 1952
Back row - Baker, Ursell, Oxborrow, C. Harrison, Hammond, Mr RW Priestland
Front row - Hockey, Peckham, Johnson, 'Doc' Freeman, B Harrison, Warr, Henley

In 1951 he graduated to the senior Hampshire Schools X1 and the *Hampshire Handbook* recorded that "Harrison was our best batsman and was deservedly top of the averages (with 45)". He confirmed his liking for the May's Bounty track with a top score of 87 the following year in a commanding win over Surrey schools and afterwards was presented with his county colours. He went on to captain the side in his final season of 1953, averaging 44 with the bat and taking eighteen wickets.

His soccer also blossomed quickly at Peter Symonds. He was small, slightly built and very fast, so his natural position was on the wing at a time when youngsters either wanted to be a centre- forward like Tommy Lawton or a winger like Stanley Matthews or Tom Finney. Bernard preferred Tom Finney because he thought him a more complete player and certainly he himself liked to score as well as create goals. He admits that he rarely passed the ball in school football. He broke all the school goalscoring records, scoring 61 goals in 24 matches in his final year in the school first X1 including 12 hattricks! In three seasons he had scored 125 goals. After his first match for Hampshire schools he

16

was approached by Ted Bates with a view to his joining Southampton, but his preference had always been for Portsmouth. He signed amateur forms for Pompey at the age of sixteen and played a few matches for their 'B' side before leaving school and averaged more than a goal a game for them.

School Sport in the Post-war Period

Bernard Harrison was one of the first grammar school boys to grasp the opportunity offered by a new focus on school sport in the immediate post-war period. This resulted from widespread concern amongst both football and cricket administrators of the need to promote participation in sport as well as to improve standards and this meshed with the new spirit of egalitarianism in the wake of the 1944 Education Act which was pushing for opportunities for all.

Schools Football

In football the FA's prime objective was to stimulate interest in amateur soccer as there were concerns that too many grammar schools were turning to rugby football. It was decided to arrange a Schools' Week at Oxford University - it quickly became an annual event with the venue alternating between Oxford and Cambridge. Seventy boys from grammar and public schools were selected each year to attend the week on the evidence of performances in inter-county matches. It was a week of trial matches leading to the selection of 'A' and 'B' teams - effectively England 'A' and 'B' sides, although not officially known as such until 1955 from when international matches were played.

Bernard was invited to attend the first such week in April 1952, staying at Worcester College Oxford, and made it through all the trial matches to play one game for the 'A' team against the famous Corinthian Casuals. For the final game against Amateur Cupholders Pegasus he lost his left-wing spot to Alan A' Court - who was to make his name with Liverpool FC - but he scored the only goal for the 'B' team in their 2-1 defeat by the England FA Youth X1.

But in 1953 he came through all the trial matches and played twice for the 'A' side - against the England Amateur X1, which included the famous Bishop Auckland player Bob Hardisty, and against Oxford University Centaurs when he turned on his speed to score a stunning individual goal after a 30 yard run.

PEGASUS - Amateur Cup Winners 1952-53
Sutcliffe, McKinna, Lunn, Brown, Laybourne, Shearwood, Carr
Tanner Pawson Saunders Alexander Vowels

English Schools Cricket

Parallel to these developments in schools' football was the impetus given to cricket in the state schools during the 1950s. MCC, doubtless aware that the public schools were no longer an inexhaustible supply-line for first-class cricket, established an enquiry into youth cricket chaired by Harry Altham who was also the first President of the English Schools Cricket Association (ESCA) in 1948/49. Before the war there had been only six Schools Cricket County Associations but by the mid-fifties most counties had been inaugurated. The ESCA arranged representative games at under 15 and under 18 levels and these competitions have spawned a number of international cricketers over subsequent years, notably Alan Knott (1962), Jack Birkenshaw (1955-56), and Ken Taylor (1950-51) and of course numerous county players. Hampshire players who played for ESCA England Schools, apart from Bernard Harrison, include Mike Barnard (1949-50), Alan Castell (1958), and Trevor Jesty (1964).

Bernard was the only schoolboy of his year nationally with the talent to capitalise doubly on these complementary initiatives by the administrators of the two national sports and to appear in both teams.

18

August 1952 was a remarkable month for him. His first match for the ESCA England Schools X1 was at the St Helen s Ground, Swansea, on the 6th and 7th in a two-day match against the Wales Secondary Schools Cricket Association. Bernard had the honour of opening the innings and recalls the long descent down the many pavilion steps and the fact that his partner was almost too nervous to hold his bat. But he must have recovered because Bernard was first out bowled for 16. Roy Woodcock, a slow left-arm bowler from Worcester RGS captained the England side and was a very talented all-round games player who won both cricket and soccer blues for Oxford University. He went on to become a schoolmaster for many years at Charterhouse. For Wales, R. W. (Bob) Barber, a very successful schoolboy cricketer and a future Lancashire, Warwickshire and England batsman and leg break and googly bowler, scored 40 not out to secure a draw.

Bernard's greatest thrill came later in the month on the 15th making his first appearance at Lords which saw him achieve second top score of 40 in a one-day match against the MCC Young Professionals. The opposition included the future Middlesex and England opener W.E. Russell and two who, like Bernie, were to join the select band of footballer/cricketers, Ray Swallow who was to go on on to play for both Derbyshire at cricket and football for Arsenal and Derby County, and Jim Standen who later represented Worcestershire as well as keeping goal for West Ham and other clubs.

(3D) LORD'S (MCC) GROUND (3D)

M.C.C. YOUNG PROFESSIONALS
v.
ENGLISH SCHOOLS C.A.
FRIDAY, AUGUST 15, 1952   (1-day Match)

ENGLISH SCHOOLS C.A.		First Innings		Second Innings
1	B. R. S. Harrison ......Hampshire	b Costello	40	
2	A. J. Davies ....Somerset	b Bick	3	
†3	G. A. Wills ....Sussex	l b w b Bick	0	
4	D. Briett...............Hampshire	b Costello	3	
5	B. Priestley.......Gloucestershire	st Day b Standen	17	
6	R. G. Woodcock ..Worcestershire	b Bick	60	
7	R. Hooker ....Middlesex	b Bick	7	
8	C. Thorne ....Surrey	b Costello	1	
9	A. F. Hill......Worcestershire	b Bick	0	
10	D. N. Fletcher ....Middlesex	c Day b Bick	3	
11	C. A. Grainger ....Hampshire	not out	6	
		B 12, l b 4, w , n-b ,	16	B , l b , w , n b
		Total	161	Total ....

FALL OF THE WICKETS
1__36   2__36   3__41   4__62   5__99   6__140   7__147   8__147   9__147   10__161
1__   2__   3__   4__   5__   6__   7__   8__   9__   10__

ANALYSIS OF BOWLING		1st Innings					2nd Innings				
Name	O.	M.	R.	W.	Wd.	N-b	O.	M.	R.	W.	Wd. N-b
Cooper	5	0	23	0	...	...	...	...	...	...	... ...
Costello	22	5	43	3	...	...	...	...	...	...	... ...
Bick	16.3	6	46	6	...	...	...	...	...	...	... ...
Standen....................	5	0	17	1	...	...	...	...	...	...	... ...
Parish	3	0	16	0	...	...	...	...	...	...	... ...

YOUNG PROFESSIONALS		First Innings		Second Innings
1	J. S. Tullett	c. Priestley .. b. Fletcher	0	
2	D. A. Bick	st. Wills.. b. Fletcher	20	
3	R. Swallow	c. Woodcock b. Hooker	6	
4	D. A. Stripp	c. Thorne. b. Hooker	12	
†5	A. G. E. Tasker	b. Grainger	2	
6	W. E. Russell	l bw. Hooker	39	
7	D. Parish	b. Fletcher	4	
8	J. B. Costello	st. Wills.. b. Fletcher	0	
9	J. A. Standen	b. Hooker	4	
*10	K. B. Day	st. Wills. b. Fletcher	6	
11	R. G. Cooper	not out	3	
		B , l-b , w , n-b	10	B , l-b , w , n-b ,
		Total	106	Total ....

FALL OF THE WICKETS
1__9   2__28   3__38   4__48   5__50   6__   7__   8__   9__   10__
1__   2__   3__   4__   5__   6__   7__   8__   9__   10__

ANALYSIS OF BOWLING		1st Innings					2nd Innings				
Name	O.	M.	R.	W.	Wd.	N-b	O.	M.	R.	W.	Wd. N-b
Grainger......................	...	...	1.	...	...		...	...	...	...	... ...
Hooker......................	...	...	4.	...	...		...	...	...	...	... ...
Fletcher......................	...	...	2.	...	...		...	...	...	...	... ...
Briett......................	3	...	2.	...	...		...	...	...	...	... ...
Thorne......................	3	...	2	...	...		...	...	...	...	... ...
Woodcock......................	2	...	2.	...	...		...	...	...	...	... ...

Umpires—E. Canning & L. Gray   † Captain   * Wicket-keeper   Scorers—P. Oakley & C. Smith
Play begins at 11   Stumps drawn at 6 (half-an-hour extra if necessary)
This card does not necessarily include the fall of the last wicket
Spectators are requested not to move from their seats during the progress of an over

ENGLISH SCHOOLS C.A. WON THE TOSS

But August 1952 had still more in store for Bernard. On the 27th and 28th he played in a Worcestershire Second X1 side which included the likes of Jack Flavell, the future England pace bowler. The match was against Northamptonshire Second X1. When Bernard came in his side was well on the way to a reasonable score so he did not expect the bowling to be out of the ordinary. But when he took strike he swears he did not see the first three deliveries that he received. He knew that they had been bowled because he heard each of them hit the wicket-keeper's gloves and saw the ball being returned round the slip cordon. The bowler was roaring in from twenty-six paces and, dragging the crease with his steel toe-cap, seemed to be delivering from about eighteen yards. Somehow Bernard survived and he went on to score 62 out of 244-6. At the tender age of seventeen he had faced a bowler who was to become one of the fastest in the history of the game, none other than Frank Tyson. And Tyson thinks that he had already reached his full pace at this time. His speed was causing problems not only to batsmen - Len Hutton was among those who had already been startled by his raw pace - but also to his close fielders. He was twenty-two, having initially been rejected by Lancashire, had lost two years to National Service, and had then attended Durham University. Interestingly he had also suffered a broken leg playing football and had decided not to try to mix the two sports. Within two years was ripping through the Australian batsmen 'Down Under'.

A year later in 1953 Bernard scored 43 at Lords against MCC Young Professionals who had more or less the same line-up as the year before. In a two-day match against the Welsh Schools played at Worcester on 19 and 20 August 1953, he opened both the batting and the bowling for the England Schools side and is able to look back with the satisfaction of having cleaned bowled two future Test players - Bob Barber, and the future England captain Tony Lewis, the latter for a duck in drawn match. He also recalls his penchant for practical jokes getting the better of him and locking Bob Barber in a lift!

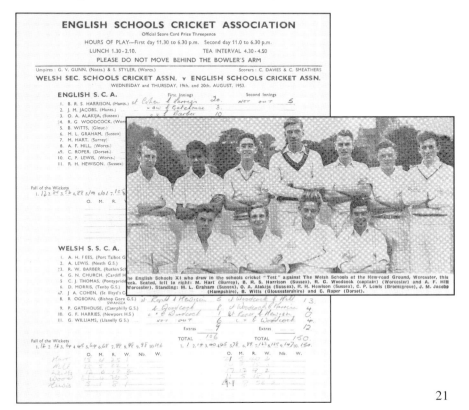

The English Schools XI who drew in the schools cricket "Test" against The Welsh Schools at the New-road Ground, Worcester, this week. Seated, left to right: M. Hart (Surrey), B. R. S. Harrison (Sussex), R. G. Woodcock (captain) (Worcester) and A. F. Hill (Hampshire); Standing: M. L. Graham (Sussex), O. A. Alakija (Sussex), R. H. Hewison (Sussex), C. P. Lewis (Bromsgrove), J. M. Jacobs (Hampshire), B. Witts (Gloucestershire) and C. Roper (Dorset).

In July he played for a Winchester and District representative side which inflicted the first defeat suffered for some years by the Hampshire Club and Ground - and he played a match-winning part in it. The opposition included Roy Marshall, the West Indian Test player who was serving a qualification period, Mervyn Burden the off spinner, and Ralph Prouton (another Hampshire footballer/cricketer, as he played for Swindon Town). Bernard - having just left school - took 4-51 including the prized wicket of Marshall and then scored 25 not out in a match-winning stand of 70 with Steve White, his cricket coach from Peter Symonds.

To complete his schooldays cricket he also appeared a month later against some of his future team-mates in a match against the Hampshire Second X1 in which the ESCA England Schools X1 just managed to preserve their unbeaten record (held since 1949) with a draw at Dean Park Bournemouth on 13 August 1953. He scored a typically a patient 33 before falling to the veteran Jim Bailey.

Clive Harrison was to follow his brother into the ESCA England Schools side. He had been groomed by his father from an early age as an off-spinner, while Bernard liked to tear in and try to bowl quickly: *"I have small hands so I couldn't really spin the ball and I had to vary it a bit. But here I was as the number one spinner with a very young Jack Birkenshaw as the number 2! I later changed to bowling seamers, but it took a long time to master the arts of medium pace."*

Bernard was an all-round athlete, school champion at both
sprint and cross-country; and 'Victor Ludorum'

22

CHAPTER TWO

A POMPEY AMATEUR... AND
AN 'AIRCRAFTSMAN FIGHTER PLOTTER'

Brought up on tales of their FA Cup-winning side of 1939, Bernard's first love in football was Portsmouth Football Club who of course remained cup-holders during the war years. His first glimpse of the professional game was to see them play Charlton Athletic in 1946 and he has memories of standing behind Sam Bartram's goal at Fratton Park. Portsmouth had built an even better side after the war and by 1950/51 were seeking to emulate Arsenal's achievement of the 1930s by winning a third championship in a row. They eventually fell away to finish in seventh place.

Amateur Terms with Pompey

Eddie Lever, who had discovered the young Jimmy Dickinson, was at this stage working with Portsmouth's reserve side while still a schoolteacher at Alton. He was known to Bernard's father, now headmaster of East Street school at Andover. He was aware of Bernard's sporting exploits as a schoolboy and he arranged for him to sign for Portsmouth as an amateur at sixteen. Bernard made three appearances in the holidays during the 1951-52 season for a very good young Pompey 'B' side which competed in the Hampshire League Division 111. He scored a couple of goals in a 4-2 win over Sandown (IOW) and then against Andover his home town's reserve side, he impressed with two more goals from left-wing in a 6-0 win. His inside partner on this occasion was Mike Barnard, like him an aspiring footballer/cricketer and a very good user of the ball at inside-forward. He was from Portsmouth Grammar School, a year or so older than Bernard, and they were also to be team-mates with Hampshire CCC. But he was to play all his soccer with Pompey, going on to make 116 first-team appearances.

Hampshire League, Division III   Monday, 14th April, 1952

ANDOVER RESERVES v. PORTSMOUTH " B "

ANDOVER RESERVES

Right				Left
	1 Prior			
	2 Dallywater	3 Burgess		
4 Tidy	5 Roughton		6 Allen	
7 Rennie	8 Conner	9 Borcher	10 Timms	11 Wildish

●

11 Harrison	10 Barnard	9 Ames	8 Kitching	7 Wilde
2. 6 Howard		5 Rutter	4 Edwards	
	3 Duggins		2 Wood	
Left	1 Bright			Right

PORTSMOUTH " B "—Blue

Won 6 - 0.

23

Another who progressed to the Football League side from this young 'B' team was Cyril Rutter, a good centre-half without frills in the traditional stopper mould.

Bernard was never one to suffer nerves at whatever level he played and, still a schoolboy, he took all this in his stride. But even he was taken aback when the following season he was named for the first time at outside-left for Portsmouth Reserves alongside players he had hero-worshipped like inside forward Johnny Gordon. This was a friendly match away to Poole Town in January 1953 which ended 1-1. The full-backs were the promising young Scotsman Alex Wilson and Phil Gunter, soon to be first team regulars as Eddie Lever - who had had taken up the managerial reins in August 1952 - began the necessary work to replace the stalwarts of the Championship winning side. Soon Jimmy Dickinson would be the sole remaining link with those great days.

After leaving school Bernard was awaiting the dreaded brown envelope to summon him to the statutory two years National Service. But he was able to fit in two games at the start of the 1953-54 season, one for Portsmouth 'A' against Fareham Town in the Hampshire League and the other a friendly for a Portsmouth X1 v. Trowbridge Town, a match in which the veteran Reg Flewin appeared at centre-half. More memorable for Bernard was to be a match during Christmas leave from the RAF on the 2nd of January 1954 when he scored a hattrick

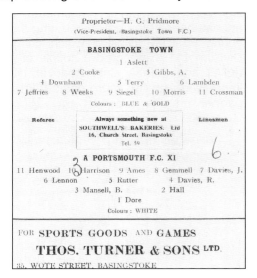

in a 6-3 victory on home territory v. Basingstoke Town at the Camrose Ground in Basingstoke.

National Service

Now his ambition for a career in professional sport was put on hold as he reported to RAF Bedford in November 1953 to have medical tests and to be kitted out. The RAF was a natural choice for grammar school boys undertaking National Service, particularly for Bernard as he had been in the RAF squadron at school. But it was with little enthusiasm that he joined his new colleagues as they were marched off to Bedford railway station and then had to stand in full kit on the train all the way to RAF Hednesford in Shropshire. The prospect was eight weeks of 'square bashing', up at 5 am in the freezing winter mornings for two hours' marching and rifle drill - without gloves - before breakfast. But he need not have worried. He soon found that talented sportsmen were much coveted - and treated with kid gloves - as there was fierce inter-camp rivalry on the sports field. On arrival the new servicemen were assembled in the main hall to be addressed by Group Captain Montgomery - cousin of the Field-Marshall - and he prefaced his address by asking all the professional footballers to fall out. Of that day's intake there were as many as 64.

Later everyone was asked to opt for their favoured activity and Bernard chose football and badminton. It transpired that he was picked to play both sports on the same day and he had to miss the badminton - with the result that he had to do a lot of explaining in order to avoid being put on a charge. The football was a reserve team match at RAF Cosford and Bernard impressed in a 5-2 win and was immediately put in the first team to play in the much-coveted RAF Cup competition. Here he met up again with Johnny Mortimore - a team-mate from the Hampshire Schools side, later the Chelsea centre-half and eventually coach to Southampton FC. Brian Farmer, full-back with Birmingham City, was another of the professionals in that RAF Hednesford team. The rest of the contingent was marched to the pitch to provide support and the senior officers were very pleased with the outcome, a 3-0 win.

By the next round Bernard had been posted to RAF Horsham St Faith in Norfolk where he remained for the rest of his service, some twenty-one months. He had really wanted a posting near home at Middle Wallop in Hampshire, an officer's station, where he had gone for four weeks to take his trade test as a "fighter plotter" but he failed and he remained an ordinary aircraftsman. Instead he found himself at Horsham St Faith where he tried to play down his sporting abilities in order to avoid a posting of long duration but his reputation had preceded him, and he was quickly commandeered for the football team. The base was intent on competing for the RAF Cup and made sure that they did not post any footballers with talent.

From then on he only ever played football - and some cricket - and he was molly-coddled while his new chums were put through it. While they marched his typical day was coffee and doughnuts for breakfast, followed by football training, then back to the billet to relax. Once after a hard day on the square they returned to find that a vindictive drill sergeant had thrown all the bedding outside - but Bernard's remained neat and untouched! Indeed he was untouchable. He never appeared on the training square again throughout the two years and he only ever put on his uniform to line up to be paid. Sometimes he felt embarrassed at his special treatment and sorry for his mates - he remembers on one occasion treating the whole billet to a meal in the NAAFI with the pound that he was receiving as a weekly retainer from Portsmouth FC. As he was receiving the standard £4 16s from the RAF, this was a considerable enhancement of his weekly wage.

As for pursuing the trade of fighter plotter, working underground to plot the position of potentially hostile aircraft, he only ever did it about five times and his incompetence was a matter for humour rather than admonishment. Luckily for Britain there were not too many enemy aircraft to worry about.

RAF Football

Football matches came thick and fast, in the East Anglian League, the Norfolk Wednesday League, the RAF Cup and various other cup competitions. He also played for the neighbouring smaller base RAF Bawburgh in the Norwich Thursday League, the RAF Junior Cup and a number of other cups. Bernard was captain and acting manager of Horsham St Faiths and was able to put together a good footballing side with a brief to bring back the RAF Cup to the base. It included goalkeeper Ray Potter who had already played for Crystal Palace and later made more than 200 appearances for WBA, Bob Heffer a winger and Alwyn Bullimore a wing-half, who both represented Norwich City, and Ian Crossley a fine centre-forward who, as a player with Grays Athletic in the Corinthian League, was to come close to selection for the England Amateur squad for the Tokyo Olympics. Bernard also met up with Roy Woodcock once more who had captained the England Schools cricket team. He was a good footballer too - he played in the Varsity match at Wembley - and added some skilful touches to the successful RAF Horsham St Faith team.

Roy remembers that with all the different league and cup competitions that there was a big accumulation of fixtures: *"Bernie thought the team should be taken off duties to concentrate on football. Everyone thought that this would never be accepted by the camp C.O. Group Captain Aitken, but Bernie could have talked the hind legs off a donkey - he could have talked for England at international level - and he went to see him and it was all agreed!".*

They won both the East Anglian League and the Norfolk Wednesday League in 1954-55 and got through to the Final of the RAF Cup, only to fall at the very last hurdle, losing 5-2 to RAF Kinross at the RAF Stadium, Uxbridge. Bernard scored in six of the seven rounds including the final, 14 goals in total. They were also runners-up in the A.O.C. Cup with the final played at Northallerton.

RAF Cup Final team
Back row - Seith, Thomas, Anderson, Potter, Woodcock, Tilley, Stewart *Front row* - Crossley, Bullimore, Harrison, Hotchkiss

Right at the end of his National Service period, in September 1955, Bernard somehow found time to make a guest appearance for Lowestoft Town in the Eastern Counties League. This was under an assumed name, although the club did not make much effort to conceal it, naming him 'L. Harrison' in the programme. Afterwards he found a £5 note - a considerable sum - stuffed into his boot.

LOWESTOFT TOWN
FOOTBALL CLUB
SEASON 1955-56

Nº 904

OFFICIAL JOURNAL 2d.
Published by the Lowestoft Town Supporters Club

Bernard made an
unofficial' appearance
for Lowestoft Town in
1955 - for 'Boot
Money'.

RAF football was
enjoyable but, apart
from the senior RAF
Cup competition,
was perhaps not
quite of the standard
to help aspiring
professional players
to develop their
game. Bernard and
Ian Crossley scored
over 200 goals
between them in the
season. Ian
Crossley remembers
that they had a race
to get to 100 goals:
*"I was on 97 and
Bernie on 96 and
then he scored four
in one match to*

Bernard with Ian Crossley
and Alwyn Bullimore

28

clinch it. I just couldn't believe the last one - the 'keeper Ray Potter threw the ball to Bernie in the right full-back position and he dribbled the whole length of the field, beating five or six players and then went round their goal-keeper TWICE before putting it in the net. I thought just who have I met here?." Their first meeting in the RAF was to lead to a life-long friendship, Ian later joining Bernard when he took on the Sports and Social side of the Portals Company and also playing cricket with Bernard for Basingstoke.

Roy Woodcock recounts a similar story: *"Bernie would never pass the ball, as he liked to hang on to it all the time. In one game against RAF West Rainham he dribbled down the right and scored, then he dribbled down the left and scored, then he dribbled down the middle and scored. In these dribbles he would often go round in circles to beat the same defenders twice. We won 10-1 with Bernie getting eight."*

RAF Cricket

Still less did the cricket provide the competitive edge required. There were some talented cricketers stationed at Horsham St Faith apart from Bernard and Roy Woodcock, including Les Brown who played for Surrey 2nd X1, but it was taken rather less seriously than the football. The main problem was the quality of the wickets since they only ever played at the airfield ground. One match sticks in Roy Woodcock's mind. Prospects for a day's play looked grim as Horsham St Faith took the field against Cranwell in the RAF Cup in overcast conditions and the visitors' opening batsman was Maurice Fenner, celebrated RAF and Combined Services cricketer over many years. *"Bernie enjoyed bowling fast off a very long a run which ended with a jump which lost all momentum, but he was still quick. He started his run-up as the rain began and by the time he reached the wicket it was pouring down like a tropical storm. Fenner did not see a thing as the ball whizzed through the rain and he was yorked first ball. We immediately ran off the field. They never recovered from the loss of their star batsman and were bowled out for just over 100 which Bernie and I knocked off to win by ten wickets."*

Back with Pompey: A Trial and Football Combination matches with Portsmouth Reserves

Bernard remained a Pompey player and during the 1954-55 season had managed to play three games for Portsmouth 'A' in the Hampshire League Division One while on leave. He was anxious to turn 'pro' with Pompey and just before his discharge he played in a trial match and then in four Football Combination games at outside-right for Portsmouth Reserves during August and September 1955. Three of the four were victories and he scored in the 2-1 win over Southend Reserves and set up three of the goals in a 5-1 win over Plymouth Reserves. But he also picked up an ankle injury. *'Stroller',* the correspondent of the *Portsmouth Football Mail* felt that the Reserves were "well stocked with talent, particularly in the forward line". He singled out Bernard for praise as a "fast tricky player and the danger man of the attack" and concluded that "it is almost certain that he will sign for the club as a professional".

Gordon Dale was on the opposite wing in two of these games, an incredibly gifted player just made for the No. 11 shirt. Bernard rated him as one of the greatest dribblers ever - virtually impossible to dispossess - a great crowd pleaser who regrettably did not fulfil his vast talent. He had become the first footballer to be transferred for £20,000 when he joined Pompey from Chesterfield in 1951.

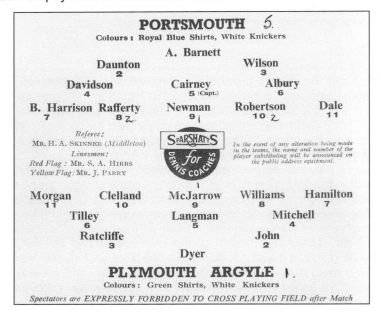

Regrettably Bernard was not to sign professional for his beloved Pompey. They asked him back for a further fortnight's trial but he felt under pressure to start earning a living as soon as he was discharged and in the meantime he went with RAF chum Ray Potter for a trial with Crystal Palace. He played well, although still carrying the ankle injury. Another good performance, this time for Crystal Palace Reserves against Arsenal 'A' in the Midweek League, and Palace stole his signature. Brother Clive thinks that Bernard's RAF service *"didn't do him any favours in career terms. He missed two important years in his development as a footballer and the friends he made there helped to determine his next move - signing for Palace."*

CHAPTER THREE

FLYING WINGER WITH CRYSTAL PALACE

"A Budding Stanley Matthews"

Bernard was not the first nor the last young player to be saddled with the "Stanley Matthews" tag. The comparison with the great Stanley was made by his manager at the Palace, Cyril Spiers, a man of vision who put his faith in developing young players. But In the late 1950s Crystal Palace was described as the club with the biggest overdraft in soccer and he was constantly under pressure to sell his young starlets. And his hottest property was twenty year-old Bernard Harrison who was soon drawing some substantial offers from First and Second Division clubs. At this stage Bernard was content that the offers were being turned down as he was enjoying life with Palace.

A series of dazzling performances on the wing and rave reviews in the press had soon attracted the scouts. When he had first come through a trial match at the start of the 1955-56 season he had impressed as "a clever ball player with a well balanced physique and a willingness to take the ball up to his opponent and beat him. His speed is deceptive, which is always a good thing for a winger, and when he was through he made ground quickly". A well known national correspondent who saw his early performances for Palace described him as the "brightest outside-right prospect for some time - and the scouts know it too". By 1957 he had progressed to the stage there was even talk of the team relying too much on a player rated "the best in the (Third) division":

"..is Harrison getting TOO MUCH of the ball? Palace forwards seem to expect him to create every chance and take the burden of most of the finishing."

And this in a side which had future England star Johnny Byrne - who made his debut as a sixteen year old in October 1956 - on the opposite wing.

Football League Division 111 - S outh v. North : October 1957

It was Bernard's selection for the Third Division South representative side which really put him in the shop window. This was for the annual match against the Northern section of the division which on this occasion was to be hosted by the Crystal Palace club who were looking for more representative games to be played at Selhurst Park. In the event they were a little disappointed with the turnout, a gate of 12,688, from an area as populous as Croydon, to see such an attractive fixture which was to feature one of their own favourites, flying winger Bernard Harrison.

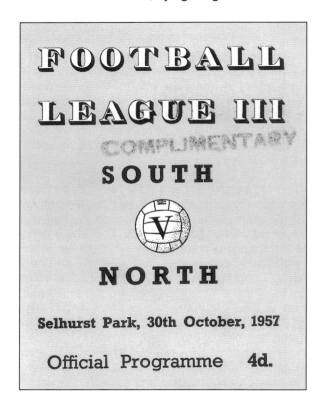

This was an historic meeting because the separate north and south sections - first established back in 1921 - were to be disbanded at the end of the 1957-58 season and the 48 clubs formed into Divisions 3 and 4. This was to be the last of the series of inter-league matches which only dated back to 1954.

The results of previous games were:

Football League 111 SOUTH V. NORTH Matches			
Year	Venue	Result	Attendance
1954-55	Reading	South 2 North 0	10,438
1955-56	Accrington	North 3 South 3	10,521
1956-57	Coventry	South 2 North 1	14,500
1956-57	Stockport	North 2 South 1	12,372

These matches were intended to promote goodwill and to foster contact between the two sections but a lot of pride was also at stake. They were also manna from heaven for the First and Second Division scouts.

Notable inclusions in the South's line-up were goalkeeper, twenty two year-old Ron Springett, who was to win more than 30 caps for England, and the experienced Alf Sherwood, a highly regarded full-back capped many times by Wales. The North's side included the England inside forward Ivor Broadis.

ROUSE DOUBTFUL FOR PORT VALE MATCH
HARRISON ATTRACTS BUT HE IS NOT FOR SALE

The match came at the right time for Bernard because he was in great form. The preceding Saturday's league game had seen him star in an impressive 3-0 win over Plymouth Argyle. One reporter enthused:

"I can understand why Palace manager Cyril Spiers gets worked up about outside-right Bernard Harrison. This boy hasn't got the lot, but he's got most of it!".

ON - the - spot inquiries were made by managers and directors of other clubs about Crystal Palace's fair - haired right-winger Bernard Harrison on Wednesday evening, following his good performance in the League representative game at Selhurst Park.

"He's not for sale," said Palace secretary-manager Mr. Spiers.

If Wright, of Colchester, who played left-wing in the South team, is worth £20,000 (that is the figure attached to his name) then the Palace could easily ask double that for Harrison—on their respective performances on Wednesday.

And Bernard did not disappoint. He carried this form into the inter-league match on the Wednesday when it was he and the captain, veteran Alf Sherwood, who were the pick of the South's side in a 2-2 draw. Arsenal and Aston Villa were among the clubs queuing up to check out his availability after the game.

THIRD DIVISION SOUTH 2

Team Manager :
Mr. J. Taylor
(Queens Park Rangers)

Reserves :
John Shepherd (Millwall)
Maurice Evans (Reading)

Colours : Red and White Stripes ; White Shorts

Ron Springett
(Q.P.R.)

BANNISTER.

2
Roy McCrohan
(Norwich)

3
Alf Sherwood
(Newport County)

4 VEITCH
Bobby McLaughlin
(Southampton)

5
Keith Harvey
(Exeter City)

6
Glen Wilson
(Brighton & Hove)

7
Bernard Harrison
(Crystal Palace)

8
Wilf Carter
(Plymouth Argyle)

SHEPHERD

9
Roy Hollis
(Southend)

10
Stanley Steele
(Port Vale)

11
Peter Wright
(Colchester)

Referee :
Mr. D. T. Blues
(Richmond)

Kick-off 7.30 p.m.

Linesmen :
D. W. Bradley (Selsdon)
(Red Flag)
Mr. C. H. Rogers
(N. Kensington) (Yellow Flag)

11
George Luke
(Hartlepools)

10
Bill Holden
(Stockport County)

9
George Stewart
(Accrington St.)

8
Ivor Broadis
(Carlisle Un.)

7
John Tomlinson
(Chesterfield)

6
Charlie Crowe
(Mansfield)

5
Wally Taylor
(Southport)

4
Jack Bertolini
(Workington)

3
Paul Feasey
(Hull City)

2
Eddie Robertsod
(Bury)

Roy MacLaren
(Bury)

Colours : White Shirts, Black Shorts

Team Manager :
Mr. Peter Jackson
(Bradford City)

Reserves :
Ronald Thompson (Carlisle)
Thomas Neill (Bury)

THIRD DIVISION NORTH 2.

Bernard then had a rather ineffective match against Newport County when he was marked by Sherwood, whom he rated as one of the best full-backs he ever encountered, but he followed it with one of the best performances he ever gave in a Crystal Palace shirt.

Crystal Palace v. Newport County -
Alf Sherwood, Wales international and rated by Bernard as one of the best full-backs he ever faced. Here he gets his head to the ball before Bernard (left) and Mike Deakin

Margate v. Crystal Palace, 16 November 1957- FA Cup First Round

PALACE MANAGE CUP WIN AT MARGATE – ONLY JUST
Harrison aids Deakin hat-trick

Drawn away to non-league Margate in the FA Cup, the Palace team was conscious of the club's poor record against non-league sides in the Cup, having lost to Finchley, Great Yarmouth and finally Bishop Auckland over recent seasons. They gave a very nervy defensive display and further embarrassment was in prospect as they went 2-1 down. Eventually they came through as lucky 3-2 winners on the strength of a hattrick by centre-forward Mike Deakin - 'with all three laid on a plate by a certain speedy and tricky right-winger'. He provided two inch perfect centres for headed goals and made the third with a square pass which simply begged to be knocked in the net. In the course of the match he had roasted his opposing full-back.

Result: **Margate 2 Crystal Palace 3** (Deakin 3) Attendance 8,200 (a ground record)
Margate Peters; Wells, Joyce; Worthington, Bonds, Watkins; Bostock, Foan, Kearns, Yeomans, Bennett.
Crystal Palace Hopgood; Greenwood, Edwards; Long, Choules, Belcher; Harrison, Cooper, Deakin, Pierce, Truett.

The local Margate paper's summation was typical of the press coverage:
Margate were unlucky but "the outstanding player on view was Bernard Harrison whose speed and artistry was responsible for the win."

Interviewed afterwards, Cyril Spiers seemed intent on bumping up the asking price with the quote that "Everyone's after Harrison but they're not going to get him. Bernard never stops thinking about the game, and like Matthews and Finney, dribbles intelligently with both feet."

Bernard swerves to avoid a challenge watched by Margate's record crowd

Those who had been thrilled by such performances would have been astonished had they known at the time that Bernard had already reached the pinnacle of his achievement as a professional footballer. So what went wrong? It was certainly difficult trying to establish a career juggling between the two sports but he also admits that - lacking an agent and the professional advice which would be available today - he made some poorly judged career moves. He perhaps thought that talent alone would see him through. He was also unlucky. Had he been allowed to join a First Division side in 1957-58 he may well have found the top flight a more suitable platform for his clever ball skills, away from the 'cloggers' who still populated the lower reaches of the Football League.

For the moment Bernard's fate as a footballer was inextricably linked to that of the manager who held him in such high regard. And also to the fate of the young Palace team. The football magazine *Soccer Star* in September 1957 ran an article on Bernard titled "the Complete Sportsman!" and concluded that "when the revival of Crystal Palace comes about I am certain Bernard Harrison will be one of the most talked about wingers in the game".

"The same wages as Stanley Matthews"

Bernard on his way to sign for Crystal Palace - he had been whisked by Rolls Royce from an 'A' team fixture to the Boardroom by the Chairman, Arthur Wait

It was Cyril Spiers who had signed Bernard while Pompey dithered after his discharge from the RAF in October 1955. He had first gone to Palace for a trial at the suggestion of goalkeeper Ray Potter who had been a National Service chum and a team-mate in RAF sides. Portsmouth's manager at the time, Eddie Lever, had concerns that, slight in build and five feet eight inches in height, he might lack the strength to cope with the rigours of the professional game. So many skilled ball-players never get to play league football because they are considered too small. While Lever asked to see Bernard in another round of trial matches, Crystal Palace needed only the evidence of one appearance in a midweek game against Arsenal 'A' team to know that they were on to a good thing. After the match the Chairman, property developer Arthur Wait, whisked him back to the club in his Rolls Royce and secured his signature at the prevailing maximum wage at that time - £15 a week in the playing season and £10 a week in the close season. Arthur Wait told him he was now on the same wages as Stanley Matthews. It was indeed a good offer to a youngster as by no means every professional footballer at that time was on the maximum. Brother Clive says Bernard was generous enough to give him £2 a week to help him to get through university.

In retrospect joining Palace was probably his first wrong career move - to join a Third Division club when he may well have been offered terms by Portsmouth of the First. Clive thinks this was a mistake for two reasons: "*Firstly he missed the opportunity to join one of the top sides of the day - and he was good enough for that. I would compare him with McManaman today. Secondly, part of the attraction was the glamorous soccer scene in the capital and this also brought the diversion of the London night-life. He got in with Johnny Byrne and others who liked a drink*".

Not that Crystal Palace was a club devoid of potential. Indeed they had some of the trappings of a big club. They owned the freehold of a ground with a capacity of 55,000 - 12, 000 under cover - with parking for 1,000 cars and, despite their lack of playing success, had a loyal following with crowds averaging over 12,000 for the last five years. Floodlights had first been introduced in 1954 and were improved a year later. But the club had only narrowly escaped having to apply for re-election at the end of 1954-55 and was losing £200 a week.

Bernard, however, very much enjoyed his time at Crystal Palace while Cyril Spiers held the reins. Unusually in soccer management, Spiers - a former Aston Villa and Spurs goalkeeper - was a "quiet and scholarly" man and Bernard found him very straight and easy to deal with. Not that as a manager he lacked resolve: he made a point of rooting out the group of players whom he referred to as the 'old brigade' whose reign had perhaps symbolically come to an end with the disastrous 4-2 home defeat by non-league Bishop Auckland in December 1954. Lacking the cheque book option, Spiers put his faith in young players and made a plea to the club's supporters to give them time to develop as a team. In the 1955-56 season the average age was reduced to twenty-two and this helped to foster a spirit of togetherness and a happy atmosphere at the club.   But wing-half Terry Long remembers this period as one of transition for the club: "*with all the young players coming in the team played very erratically, winning by many goals in one match only to lose the next to a team we should have beaten". So*on some commentators began to suggest that Palace needed at least one more experienced head to guide the youngsters.

A Footballer's Lot

It was a diminutive and boyish looking Bernard who had turned up for his first day's training and - with his grammar school background - he cut a rather unlikely figure as a professional footballer.   Then,   as now, footballers tended to be from working class families and to have   limited   educational attainment. But his two years in National Service had brought him into contact with a broader social

With flat-mates Mike Deakin (left), Gwyn Evans and landlord Johnny Bull (centre)

spectrum and he quickly settled into his new life. He was naturally very gregarious and also excelled at the things footballers tended to do to while away the time when not training - cards, snooker etc. - and this helped. He went into digs near Selhurst Park initially with team-mates Mike Deakin and Gwyn Evans.

The training staff at Palace were, like Spiers himself, easy men to work with - Jack Blackman,"Jesse" Willard, and Tom Brolly - but the training methods of the English game remained primitive compared to the new methods being pioneered in countries like Austria and Hungary.

"JESSE" WILLARD

The Training Team at Palace

TOM BROLLY

JACK BLACKMAN

(Crystal Palace FC Annual 1957-58)

Looking back, however, Bernard tends to confirm the stereotypical view that we have of football training at that time - a monotonous diet of lapping the pitch, jogging and cross-country running. Charles Hughes at Loughborough University had carried out a survey of English League clubs' training methods and found that a week's training typically consisted of no less than 185 minutes of lapping out of a total training time of 400 minutes, while ball work averaged less than 90 minutes and could be as little as 30 minutes.

Palace trained from ten until twelve each morning, with extra sessions in the afternoon following a bad result. After the jogging and lapping the players also worked in threes to practice ball skills with some limited work on set pieces and finished with a six-a-side match. For one season the players had to run up and down the terraces with packs on their backs, not a popular innovation!

Palace players listen attentively to trainer Jack Blackman (from the left) Cooper, Long, Harrison, Edwards, McDonald, Rouse, Murray, Deakin and Berry

Some players did not relish the cross-country running and found all sorts of devious means to avoid it including hitching rides on milk floats! Bernard had no such problems, having been the school cross-country record holder (5 miles in 25 minutes) and he was also the fastest sprinter in the Palace squad, having clocked 10.5 for 100 yards. Indeed Joe Hulme via his column in the *People* put forward the suggestion of running a competition at White City to find the fastest sprinter in football, and challenged people to find a footballer to match Bernard's speed. In the event he only met his match when he joined Southampton and came up against John Sydenham.

Bernard often spent the afternoon practising with Johnny Byrne who became a great friend, sending over crosses for Johnny to perfect his already impressive volleying technique. Otherwise they joined the other unmarried players to while away the time playing snooker and cards for high stakes. Bernard reckons that one year he earned as much from this as he did from his football! An outstanding badminton player, he also played in the top London league while with Palace. At school he had been a county player and an all-England semi-finalist in the doubles with Bob Grinstead, and had reached the last eight in the singles. Brother Clive was an even better badminton player and went on to captain Oxford University against Cambridge.

CRYSTAL PALACE PLAYERS 1957-58
(all photos from the Club Annual)

Like Bernard, Terry Long came from a grammar school background. He was a loyal servant to Palace as a defender and later a coach with George Graham at Arsenal.

TERRY LONG

BERNARD HARRISON

Barry Pierce was an inside-forward rated by Bernard as the best header of a ball he ever played with. Later joined Millwall.

BARRY PIERCE

42

ALFIE NOAKES

Alfie Noakes was a useful full-back who made 195 appearances for Palace before moving on to Portsmouth

MIKE DEAKIN

Mike Deakin came from the Midlands and was a strong centre-forward who scored 56 goals for Palace in 143 matches before moving to Northampton Town.

RAY POTTER

Instrumental in getting Bernard to join Palace, Ray Potter kept goal in just 44 games before spending eight successful seasons at West Brom.

VIC ROUSE

Vic Rouse was a fine goal-keeper who made 238 appearances for Palace, winning an international cap for Wales while playing in the Third Division.

Jimmy Belcher was a skilful wing-half or inside-forward for Palace in the 1954-57 period (22 goals in 128 matches) before being signed by Alf Ramsey for Ipswich Town. While with Palace he played for Third Division 111 South against the North in 1956-57.

Len Choules was a one club player, making 258 appearances at centre-half from 1952 to 1961. Rated by Bernard as a very good centre-half, six feet tall but slightly built for a defender and very quick.

The Crystal Palace star product who played 203 games for the club with 85 goals before moving to West Ham for a record fee of £65,000. He won an FA Cup winners' medal with West Ham but missed the European Cup Winners Cup Final victory because of a knee injury. He won fewer England caps (11) than his ability merited, missing out on the 1966 World Cup campaign. He returned briefly to Palace in 1967. He emigrated to South Africa where he died in 1999

Brother of ill-fated 'Busby Babe' Johnny Berry, Peter was a talented ball player and a versatile forward who played 151 games for Crystal Palace, scoring 27 goals, before being taken to Ipswich Town by Alf Ramsey.

Roy Greenwood was a whole-hearted strong-tackling full-back, another one-club man. Later coached and managed in South Africa.

League Debut with a touch of 'flu

Back on the football pitch, in his first season (1955-56) he was largely confined to Reserve team matches in the Football Combination. He remembers a 6-0 thrashing by a Leicester City reserve side which included the veteran Matt Gillies, Howard Riley and Colin Appleton who were both in the team which later won promotion through the divisions to the top flight and also reached the FA Cup final in 1961, and Tony Knapp (later of Southampton). He played some first team friendly matches and then came the call to say that Mike Deakin was injured so he was to travel with the first team to Colchester. Bernard faced a dilemma. Did he reveal that he had a touch of '**flu** and miss his league debut? He kept quiet and he played well in a 4-2 win.

Colchester
United

1955-56

COLCHESTER UNITED FOOTBALL CLUB · TELEPHONE 4042

OFFICIAL PROGRAMME   **PRICE THREEPENCE**

Copyright reserved COMPLIMENTARY

But then he was back in the Reserves for his most difficult match of the season v. Southampton, marked by Bill Ellerington, a full-back with two England caps and the best that Bernard had come up against thus far. A first team friendly against Fulham at the end of the season gave Bernard his first brush with Johnny Haynes who had just been named in the England side to play Scotland. To this day he regards Haynes as the best long passer with either foot that he ever encountered.

The Age of Wingers

When Bernard returned from cricket at the beginning of 1956-57 he went straight into the first team and by the end of the season had played 53 first team matches including the friendlies, mostly in his preferred position of outside-right. This was still very much the age of wingers, and there was a certain romanticism attached to the number 7 shirt - romanticism which had built around the tradition of great wingers in the British game, a tradition stretching from Matthews as far back as Billy Meredith.

CRYSTAL PALACE F.C. — 1956-57
BACK ROW *(l. to r.)* **J. Edwards : J. Belcher : R. Potter : T. Long : L. Charles : A. Noakes**
FRONT ROW *(l. to r.)* **B. Harrison : P. Berry : M. Deakin : S. Cooper : B. Pierce**

In his early days at Palace Bernard won a contest for the right-wing berth with Peter Berry - brother of Johnny, one of the 'Busby Babes' who was to be badly injured in the Munich air disaster - but Berry was to prove himself a versatile performer all across the front line. The Palace crowd really took to Bernard, reserving a special cheer for him as he ran onto the pitch, and throughout his sporting life he had something of the showman about him. He liked to perform for the fans. His friend from RAF days Ian Crossley says he only realised this trait in Bernard much

47

later: *"When we were playing for Portals in the Hampshire League I was curious why he liked to switch wings at half-time. Then I twigged it. He wanted to play on the side where the crowd was."*

At Palace Bernard mostly played out wide on the right and when he received the ball he had the freedom to take on his full-back. For team-mate Terry Long it is Bernard's speed off the mark that hangs in the memory: *"he was quick, hard working and a good goalscorer, and generally a good team player."* He certainly liked to use his speed - to play the ball one side of the full-back and race round the other, a manouevre which got the crowd going - but he was not just a one dimensional player, the sort whom professionals used to describe as simply "fast without the ball". He knew how to use his speed on the football field. He was a clever dribbler with both feet, keeping the ball close, teasing the full-back by showing him enough of the ball to draw a challenge before accelerating away usually on the outside. Once he was away he was never caught and he had the ability to deliver pinpoint crosses from the right. Not that the very heavy playing surface at Selhurst Park - typical of pitches generally around this time - offered any encouragement to the more intricate ball players like Bernard. Also it was not long before defences double banked to reduce his threat and he found himself facing a defensive wing-half as well as the full-back. When he switched wings he was never as happy on the left flank from where he tended to drive in crosses rather than flight them. Ian Crossley played a few games for Crystal Palace Reserves at this time and recalls watching the first team against Leicester City: *"They had clearly detailed the left-back to kick Bernard into the stands, but he couldn't catch him. He undoubtedly had all he skills, the twinkling feet."*

Bernard (second from left) tries to keep on his toes in a typical mud bath at Selhurst Park

The Brentford goal-keeper saves Bernard's shot with his feet at Selhurst Park in 1957

His preferred inside partner was Peter Berry but he also linked up well with Jimmy Belcher, wing-half or inside-forward, both of them fine ball players. At their best their approach play, as they combined and interchanged, had the press corps purring in admiration, referring to them as that "mystifying old firm of Berry and Harrison" after they had teased and mesmerised the Brentford defence. But when Johnny McNichol - a fine passer of the ball - arrived from Chelsea, Bernard nevertheless feels he became less effective as he was starved of the ball. Both Berry and Belcher were later signed by the canny Alf Ramsey for Ipswich Town.

THE CRYSTAL PALACE FORWARD LINE
- in Training before an FA Cup tie

The 'Hard Men'

But the early part of his first full season of league football also exposed Bernard to the sort of treatment he could expect from hard-bitten full-backs who could not cope with his speed. He encountered two of the well-known 'cloggers' of the Division in Stan Anslow of Millwall and Ray Reeves of Reading. Bernard had made the mistake of watching Anslow play at Brighton which had confirmed his hard man reputation and it was with some trepidation that he lined up against him when Palace came to play Millwall. Early on he nullified Bernard's threat by stamping on his ankle with the parting shot "that's finished you". Reeves, the Reading left-back, was very slow on the turn and set out to slow down his opposing winger with some early punishment. Terry Paine of Southampton, the best winger in the Division, was petrified of him and tended to 'disappear' when playing at Reading. Palace had their own hard man, too, in Roy Greenwood a brave player who was prepared to put his head where others feared to put a boot. Like many such players he was a very nice man off the pitch. Later at Southampton Bernard was to team up with Cliff Huxford, ex-Chelsea wing-half, who as a ruthless tackler was held in awe even by that more celebrated hard man 'Chopper' Harris.

The Likely Lads - with Alfie Noakes (left) and
George Cooper in a Torquay night club

50

Classy Defenders

The Division also boasted some good footballing full-backs. These included Tommy Trayner of Southampton, an Eire international, who was strong, fairly fast with a good left foot. Also Alf Sherwood of Newport County, a Welsh international, was in Bernard's estimation a great defender who knew just the right moment to challenge and used his body strength to good effect to bar the route down the touchline. But probably the best left-back he ever faced was Jim Langley of Fulham, who earned three caps for England. He had pace, was good in possession, and was an excellent tackler who was difficult to pass on either side despite being very left-sided. As for central defenders he rated the young Charlie Hurley, then with Millwall and later more famously with Sunderland, as amongst the best.

Crystal Palace v. Brentford, 12th December 1956 - FA Cup Second round replay

In 1956-57, too, he sampled the exciting atmosphere unique to the FA Cup. After a 1-1 draw at Brentford, Bernard treated a 23,000 Selhurst Park crowd to a superb exhibition of wing play as Palace won the replay 3-2 after extra time. He created all three of a hattrick of headers by Barry Pierce.

Result: **Crystal Palace 3** (Pierce 3) **Brentford 2** (after extra time) Attendance 23,137.
Crystal Palace Potter; Edwards, McDonald; Long, Choules, Noakes; Harrison, Belcher, Berry, Pierce, Deakin
Brentford Cakebread; Dargie, Tickrdge; Coote, Bragg, Peplow; Parsons, Morgan, Francis, Towers, Newcombe.

But then Palace lost in next round to Millwall in a mud bath at the Den, watched by a crowd of 26,790. Perhaps inevitably Spiers' young team lacked consistency. Palace, who had to seek re-election at the end of 1955-56, at least avoided that indignity again by climbing to 20th in Division 3 (South) in 1956-57. But now they needed to finish in the top half of the table after the 1957-58 campaign to avoid dropping to the Fourth Division which was to come into being for the following season.

Bernard's form had hit the heights earlier in the 1957/58 season culminating in his selection for the South v. North, but now it took a dip and he lost confidence. He still took players on but he started to lose the ball and the crowd who had earlier cheered him now started to get on his back. Then as now it was always the gifted players - those who have the talent to try the unexpected - who were scapegoats when things turned against a team. The percentage players, the metronomes, who only ever play safe passes, somehow take refuge within their own mediocrity. Bernard's style of play, by contrast, was to commit defenders and to take risks and this meant he was always noticed.

Brighton and Hove Albion v. Crystal Palace, 22 March 1958 - Football League Division 3 (South)

Towards the end of the season he was once again the pick of the forward line. In the run-in to the end of this vital campaign, a 20,000 crowd at the Goldstone Ground saw him put on what was called a "gilt-edged show" and score a fine goal. Palace took a two-goal lead over promotion chasing Brighton, only brought back to level terms by the home side in the last twenty minutes with goals from Dave Sexton - later a fine coach and a manager of Chelsea and Manchester United - and another footballer/cricketer Dennis Foreman. But then with seconds of injury time left Bernard slipped in possession and as he fell he handled the ball. The resultant free kick led to a melee in the Palace area, the Brighton centre-forward Harburn miskicked and the ball rolled into the net off the post and Brighton had somehow snatched a dramatic 3-2 victory. For Palace this was a dispiriting defeat after outplaying Brighton for most of the match in a superb performance. Returning to the dressing room, Bernard remembers that two or three players were in tears and there was a feeling that Cyril Spiers would face the sack.

Result: **Brighton & Hove Albion 3 Crystal Palace 2** (Harrison, Pierce)
Attendance 19,611
Brighton Gill; Tennant, Ellis; Bates, Whitfield, Wilson; Gordon, Sexton, Harburn, Foreman, Howard.
Crystal Palace Rouse; Greenwood, Noakes; Long, Choules, Sanders; Harrison, McNichol, Berry, Pierce, Collins.

While Brighton went on to head the league and to win promotion to Division Two, Palace finished in 14th spot when 12th place - a difference of four points - would have been enough to take them into the new Third Division. They had made progress over the club's performance in recent seasons but perhaps the acid test had come just too soon for this young and emerging side. In June 1958 the club sadly parted company with Cyril Spiers and from this point it was probably only a matter of time before Bernard followed him.

Crystal Palace v. Brighton at Selhurst Park

The Brighton keeper punches clear, challenged by Mike Deakin,
watched by Bernard (left)

A Rare Sight - Bernard airborne for a heading duel.

Floodlit Friendlies at Selhurst Park

The team may have lacked consistency in the league but the fans at Selhurst Park did not lack for entertainment in this period. Friendly games were an important ingredient in the football mix in the days before televised football. Crystal Palace, a club very proud of its facilities, was able to stage some high profile friendly fixtures under floodlights, mostly at the end of the season, which provided fine entertainment and some remarkable 'brushes with the greats' for the players.

Crystal Palace v. Army X1, Monday 8th October 1956

War-time football produced some remarkable army team line-ups, but scarcely moreso than the National Service period when the Army side was able to field the cream of England's young players. The team they put out for this match was virtually the England Under 23 team. The line-up in retrospect is both remarkable and poignant, including as it does two of the 'Busby Babes' who were to perish in the Munich aircrash, Duncan Edwards and Eddie Coleman, and two others who survived - Bobby Charlton and Billy Foulkes.

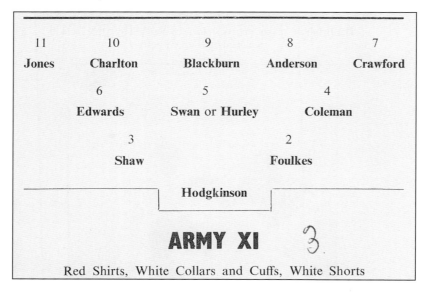

Bernard scored a goal in a 3-3 draw and particularly remembers Duncan Edwards for his commanding play at left-half and Cliff Jones who was to become one of the greatest wingers of all time for Spurs and Wales.

Pen Portraits of the

ARMY XI

Hodgkinson (*Goalkeeper*)
Royal Signals and Sheffield United. A most promising Goalkeeper who appeared for the Sheffield United first team on several occasions last year. Played for England under 23's recently.

Foulkes (*Right Back*)
R.A.S.C. and Manchester United. One of the outstanding products of the United junior system. In company with team mates Ray Wood and Roger Byrne has represented England several times. Has played regularly for his Club's League side this season.

Shaw (*Left Back*)
Royal Signals and Sheffield United. Gained England under 23's Cap last season. A back with a very promising future.

Coleman (*Right Half*)
Royal Signals and Manchester United. One of the Manchester United babes with a future. Diminutive but tireless and clever. Has played regularly for his Club's League side this season.

Swan (*Centre Half*)
Royal Signals and Sheffield Wednesday. A well-built player who should make his name before long. Of good physique with tireless energy. Has appeared in his Club's League side.

or

Hurley (*Centre Half*)
Army Catering Corps and Millwall. A young player of great promise. Selected for Eire last season, but missed his Cap through injury.

Edwards (*Left Half*)
R.A.O.C. and Manchester United. Schoolboy International, Youth International, England under 23's, " B " International, and has been capped for his country on several occasions. Gained all these honours before the age of 19. Plays regularly for his Club's League side.

Crawford (*Outside Right*)
Camerons and Hearts. A speedy shooting winger who can play on either wing. Scored in last season's Scottish Cup Final. Plays regularly for his Club's League side.

Anderson (*Inside Right*)
Royal Tank Regiment and Sunderland. Player who looks to have a really great future ; played for England under 23's side at Fratton Park, Portsmouth, against Denmark last season, and was travelling reserve for England in Denmark. Made his League debut for Sunderland while in his 'teens, this being in 1953. Has also played for the England " B " side.

Blackburn (*Centre Forward*)
Royal Artillery and West Ham United. A strong centre-forward with a good turn of speed. Has played for his Club's League side this season.

Charlton (*Inside Left*)
R.A.O.C. and Manchester United. A player for whom a great future is predicted. Plays for his Club in the Central League. Scored over 40 goals last season.

Jones (*Outside Left*)
Royal Horse Guards and Swansea. Speedy and clever winger. Welsh International.

Another annual event, the visit of the International Managers X1, was regarded as the highlight. It provided equally remarkable team line-ups, although of players and managers at the veteran stage.

Crystal Palace v. International Managers' X1, Monday 29th October 1956

Cyril Spiers in his programme notes reminded fans of the match the previous year when Jimmy Hagan, a bit of a maestro and still a Sheffield United player at age 38, had put on a great show and scored four goals. Spiers promised "entertainment one rarely sees these days - pure scientific football with the ball being made to do the work."

Directors :

J. R. DUNSTER (Chairman)   V. ERCOLONI (Vice-Chairman)
R. SHRAGER   A. J. WAIT
Secretary-Manager : CYRIL SPIERS   Trainer : J. BLACKMAN
Medical Officer : P. SOMMERVILLE, M.B., Ch.B.   Asst. Trainer : T. BROLLY

CLUB NOTES
by
Cyril Spiers

We are all naturally disappointed that Stanley Matthews is prevented once more from being with us this evening. Stanley is selected to play for the Football League against Ireland on Wednesday.

Once again we welcome these famous Managers and Players, and thank them for the great compliment they have paid us by appearing this evening.

All these players have had long and distinguished playing careers and most of them are now successful Managers ; but, make no mistake about it, they still love to strip off and play whenever the opportunity occurs.

You have seen the football they are capable of—the easy way they make the ball do the work, and the accuracy of the final effort. Remember Jimmy Hagen's four goals last Season ?—four half-chances being made into four grand goals.

Now sit back and let us enjoy this football feast, for that is what it will be, I am sure.

OFFICIAL PROGRAMME – Threepence

Monday, 29th October, 1956

56

Bernard certainly confirms that the Palace defenders found it difficult to get a touch of the ball despite the advanced age of some of the veterans! Stanley Matthews was originally down to play, but had been picked for the English League v. Irish League two days later, so he had to withdraw. Bernard scored in the 4-3 defeat and was marked by Laurie Scott, the former Arsenal and England full-back, who had also played a few games for Crystal Palace in 1951-52. Two footballer/cricketers Arthur Milton and Willie Watson appeared and other very notable inclusions were Peter Doherty, famous Northern Ireland inside-forward, and Bill Shankley who had by now started in management with Huddersfield Town.

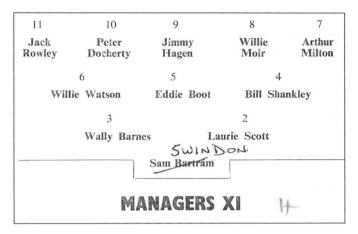

Southern Floodlight Challenge Cup

There was also competitive football under floodlights in a new cup competition started in the 1955-56 season. There were some teething problems because, although the Football Association had agreed, the Football League would not sanction member clubs making extra payments to players. Some clubs proceeded anyway and the competition got underway with only ten clubs participating, Palace losing to West Ham who went on to win the Final against Aldershot. The Football League relaxed its rules for the following season and the competition expanded to include four First Division clubs, two from the Second, and seven from the Third Division (South). These were, in addition to Crystal Palace, Arsenal, Charlton Athletic, Chelsea, Luton Town, Leyton Orient, West Ham United, Aldershot, Brentford, Millwall, Queens Park Rangers, Reading and Watford. Three of the clubs lacked floodlight facilities and so had to play all their matches away from home.

Palace were to contest the Final with Arsenal in 1958-59, when Bernard had to watch from the stand as they lost 2-1 in front of a 32,000 crowd, but his first appearance in the competition was a four goals to nil defeat to the Gunners' first team in October 1956.

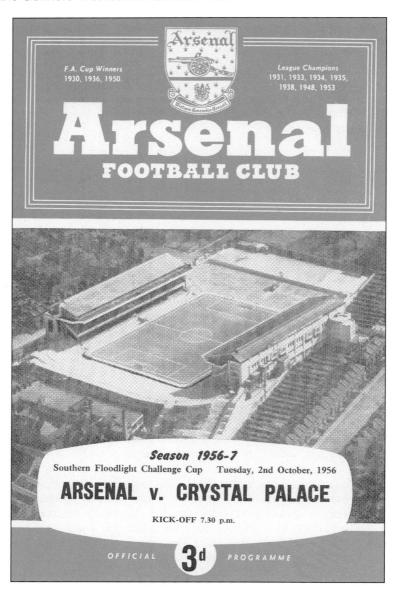

CRYSTAL PALACE PLAYERS AND STAFF

Back Row : *Left to Right.* **B. Collins, D. Ash, A. Collins, R. Farrell, W. Denton, J. Edwards, J. Sanders, A. Brown, A. Proudler.** **Second Row :** *Left to Right.* **J. Willard, A. Noakes, R. Greenwood, B. Harrison, V. Rouse, R. Hopgood, T. Long, B. Pierce, L. Choules, M. Deakin, T. Brolly** (*Asst. Trainer*). **Front Row:** *Left to Right.* **B. Driscoll, G. Truett, R. Brett, J. Blackman** (*Trainer*), **G. Smith** (*Manager*), **Miss M. Montague** (*Secretary*), **J. McNichol, J. Byrne, G. Cooper**

Palace had approached Arthur Rowe, much respected coach and manager of the famous 'push and run' Spurs side, with a view to his taking the vacant managerial position. But he had given up football due to ill health and on his recommendation Palace turned to George Smith, although Arthur Rowe did join him as Assistant Manager in November 1958. Smith was an outspoken and abrasive former PT instructor in the Army whom had been nicknamed 'the Sergeant Major' as a coach at Sheffield United. He had won a wartime International cap for England as a centre-half. He was a very different character from either Cyril Spiers or Arthur Rowe who were much more friendly and approachable. All bluster, he said that if promotion was not achieved within two years he would resign (which he was to do in April 1960, with Arthur Rowe succeeding him).

The new Team Manager George Smith who was soon at loggerheads with Bernard

He took an immediate dislike to Bernard Harrison both as a person - he thought him too clever by half - and as a footballer. While Bernard liked to introduce innovative ideas at team talks such as how to bring more flexibility to their attacking play, Smith was more concerned to get his most creative player to tackle back. He was to accuse him of not trying hard enough. Bernard preferred to conserve his energies for teasing runs down the touchline and will admit that, towards the end of the football season, he had half an eye on the forthcoming cricket season and was careful to avoid injury. But Smith's antagonism ran deeper than that. He was one of a breed of coaches emerging from FA courses around this time who, obsessed with work-rate, were eventually to erase wingers from the English game for a generation. Bernard was actually fiercely competitive, but his high degree of natural ability at all games meant that he made things look easy and this was emphasised because he enjoyed creating this impression. Football coaches, however, tended to look primarily for evidence of sweat expended.

At the start of the 1958-59 season George Smith wanted to show he meant business and he demanded Bernard's early recall from cricket. The first match in the Fourth Division was a memorable one, a 6-2 victory at Selhurst Park over Crewe Alexandra, with both Byrne - now settled at inside-left - and Deakin each netting a hattrick.

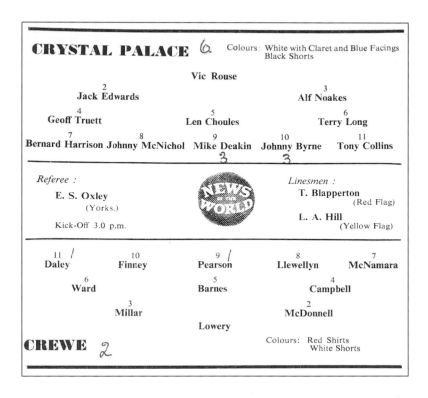

CRYSTAL PALACE 6. Colours: White with Claret and Blue Facings
Black Shorts

Vic Rouse

2
Jack Edwards

3
Alf Noakes

4
Geoff Truett

5
Len Choules

6
Terry Long

7
Bernard Harrison

8
Johnny McNichol

9
Mike Deakin
3

10
Johnny Byrne
3

11
Tony Collins

Referee :
E. S. Oxley
(Yorks.)

Kick-Off 3.0 p.m.

NEWS OF THE WORLD

Linesmen :
T. Blapperton
(Red Flag)

L. A. Hill
(Yellow Flag)

11
Daley

10
Finney

9
Pearson

8
Llewellyn

7
McNamara

6
Ward

5
Barnes

4
Campbell

3
Millar

Lowery

2
McDonnell

CREWE 2 Colours: Red Shirts
White Shorts

Despite the drop to Division 4 the crowd remained loyal with 13,500 attending the first match of the season. This was followed by an exciting 3-3 home draw v. Chester City, with more goals from Deakin and Byrne (2), the crowd rising to 18,000 for this evening fixture. However this early promise dissipated somewhat with a 3-0 defeat at Northampton, where the programme notes recorded that "Bernard Harrison's outstanding efforts came to naught", and then a 3-2 defeat in the return match at Chester. Consecutive draws at home to Workington and away to Watford and York followed.

Two successive home wins against Watford and Bradford saw Bernard hit his very best form once more.

Crystal Palace v. Watford, 17th September 1958 - Football League Division 1V

This midweek evening match sent a 16,000 crowd home happy. Bernard combined well on the right with wing-half McNichol, making one goal and scoring another with his head as his "wizardry" drew familiar Matthews comparisons from the press corp. *"The 23-year old outside -right's natural skill and ability to sell the dummy, coupled with Johnny McNichol's precision passes could put him among the country's top wingers".*

Result **Crystal Palace 3** (Truett, Byrne, Harrison) **Watford 0** Attendance 16,034
Crystal Palace Rouse; Edwards, Noakes; Truett, Choules, Long; Harrison, McNichol, Deakin, Byrne, Collins.
Watford Collins; Bell, Harrop; Catleugh, McNeice, Meadows; Gavin, Gordon, Howfield, Ching, Devins.

Crystal Palace v. Bradford 20th September 1958 - Football League Division 1V

Teams from the former northern section of the old Third Division had been having a tough time of it in Divison Four thus far and Bradford were largely out-classed by Palace. Another good crowd saw Bernard, again well prompted by McNichol, provide a stream of crosses, only two of which were put away - one by Deakin and one by Collins. McNichol also missed a penalty and went close on a number of other occasions. Again the newspapers waxed lyrical:

" Highlight of this game was the brilliant display by outside-right Bernard Harrison - slightly built, blond, so often barracked by sections of the Selhurst Park crowd last season. He showed amazing bursts of speed, coupled with good ball control and hard shooting and gave Bradford left-back Bates an unhappy afternoon."

The crowd took exception to some of Bradford's tackling which was interestingly described by the *Croydon Times* as " the usual Northern rough-and -tumble tactics"!
Result **Crystal Palace 2** (Collins, Deakin) **Bradford 0** Attendance 14,134
Crystal Palace Rouse; Edwards, Noakes; Truett, Choules, Long; Harrison, McNichol, Deakin, Byrne, Collins.
Bradford Routledge; Suddards, Bates; Brims, Williams, Atkinson; Heenan, Ward, Buchanan, Booth, Kendall.

It seems scarcely credible after such reviews that a mere five matches later he was languishing in the Reserves. As for the team the inconsistency characteristic of the Spiers' period was once more in evidence as these two classy performances by Palace were followed by a disappointing 4-1 reverse at Hartlepool, although Bernard sustained his form as the "live-wire of the attack". A narrow away victory at Port Vale with Bernard well below his best was followed by another defeat by Hartlepool. George Smith was losing patience with his team. He felt that certain players were not pulling their weight and at times he was abusive. At the next game, at the Den, he really laid into the side at half-time, despite their 1-0 lead over Millwall, watched by a 20,000 crowd. His attitude contributed to the eventual 2-1 defeat.

Bernard outstrips Millwall defenders Bob Humphries (centre) and Harold Redmond (right). The former had joined the RAF on the same day as Bernard, while the latter was a former Palace team-mate.

After the next match, a 1-0 home win over Southport, Smith phoned Bernard at his digs, shouted "you're dropped" and, without further explanation, slammed the receiver down. He was replaced at No. 7 initially by Carlo Nastri, one of the smallest players ever to play professional football, and then by Gerald Priestley. Neither was to make a career at Palace who eventually finished in seventh place.

From then on he was condemned to the Reserves, usually at outside-left which he hated, except for a first team friendly v. Sutton and an FA Cup victory over Ashford Town. At the end of the season he was forced to play until the bitter end so that he could not rejoin the Hampshire cricket team as early as he wanted. He was made available for transfer and back in Southampton Ted Bates was asking him to sign for the Saints.

Having heard nothing from Palace during the close season he began to get worried. When he contacted the club George Smith was on holiday, but Arthur Rowe said that there had been enquiries from other clubs. On his return Smith was clearly intent on making Bernard's departure as difficult as possible, denying the interest from other clubs. So with few other options and the season fast approaching, eventually Ted Bates got his man for an undisclosed fee. The Saints were a progressive club on the way up but it was not the glamorous move that would have been open to Bernard before George Smith's arrival on the scene. It was very convenient, given that Southampton was also the headquarters of Hampshire County Cricket Club, but Saints already had in Terry Paine one of the best right-wingers in the country and also an emerging Young England player soon to make the number 11 shirt his own, John Sydenham.

Wedding Day - from the left Alec Moyse (brother-in-law), Arthur Proudler, Bernard, bride Doris, Mike Deakin, Johnny Byrne, Barry Pierce, and Ronnie Brett

Letter from Assistant Manager Arthur Rowe about Bernard's likely transfer

As Bernard left Crystal Palace Smith finally admitted that he had "ruined" him as a footballer in trying to get him to change the way he played. Indeed a number of the young players who had emerged under Cyril Spiers and had promised so much, including Deakin, Berry and Belcher, were soon to drift away from Palace and, like Bernard, were never to reach their full potential as footballers.

CHAPTER FOUR

BRIEFLY A 'SAINT'

Playing for Crystal Palace against Southampton

Whilst with Crystal Palace Bernard had always reserved good performances for the Southampton match and Ted Bates had retained that early interest in him first kindled way back in Hampshire schools football. His first appearance against the Saints had been in a reserve team match back in 1956 when Palace had triumphed 3-1 in the Football Combination at the Dell, with Bernard scoring one of the goals.

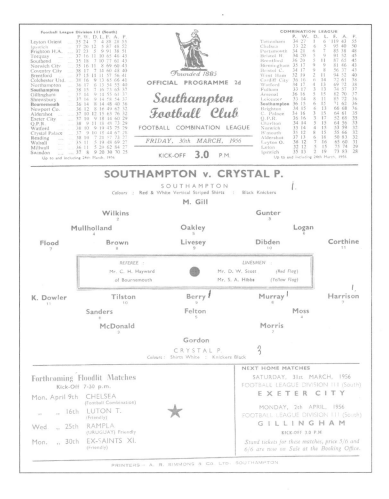

Six months later he had progressed to the Palace first team and was the pick of the forwards as the Londoners went down 3-0 to Saints with goals from Tommy Mulgrew, Derek Reeves and Jimmy Shields, the Northern Ireland international whose league career was to be ended when he suffered a broken leg the following year.

It was in 1957-58 that Bernard inflicted the most telling damage on the free-scoring Saints, playing a leading role as they were despatched from the FA Cup in the second round at Selhurst Park.

Crystal Palace v Southampton, 7 December 1957 - FA Cup second round

Crystal Palace had put their stamp on this game right from the outset, Peter Berry twice feeding Bernard who outran the Saints' defence to put in dangerous crosses. Only their finishing had let them down as their fast raids kept the Southampton defence at full stretch. Berry at last capped a fine display with a classic goal in the second half. Despite a late Southampton rally led by the experienced Don Roper, who had returned to the south coast club after nearly ten successful years with Arsenal, Palace were more than worthy of their one goal win.

Call 'Saints' sinners after this Cup waste

by DAVID JACK

CRYSTAL PALACE ... 1   SOUTHAMPTON ... 0

PETER BERRY and Bernard Harrison, Crystal Palace centre-forward and outside right, have an almost uncanny understanding on the football field. Their switching and scheming at speed put Southampton out of the game at Selhurst Park

TIME after time the Berry-Harrison manoeuvring spreadeagled the Saints' defence, and if the Palace shooting had been better the goals would have come sooner to save home supporters their anxiety for most of the game.

Although the score suggests it was a close affair, I thought Palace had all the answers from start to finish. Southampton, on this form, are a very ordinary team and they'll have to show a lot of improvement if they are not going to be saddled with the indignity of Fourth Division football as well as this early Cup exit.

It came in the 71st minute when Pierce put Berry through beautifully. Thn centre-forward shot at goalkeeper Christie and the ball was deflected to Traynor. I expected it to be gratefully booted over the stand but Traynor gave Berry a second bite at the cherry and he made no mistake this time.

Three minutes later Harrison shot wide after the best move of the game had been conjured up between himself and Berry. It would have been a goal worth remembering had it gone in.

Still, one was enough to sink a most disappointing Saints team. The defence coped reasonably well, but what a feeble forward line !

Result **Crystal Palace 1** (Berry) **Southampton 0** Attendance 14,794
Crystal Palace Rouse; Edwards, Greenwood; Belcher, Choules, Sanders; Harrison, Long, Berry, Pierce, Collins.
Southampton Christie; Page, Traynor; McLaughlin, Parker, Logan; Paine, Roper, Reeves, Mugrew, Hoskins.

Palace were to make a disappointing exit in the following round -losing 1-0 to Ipswich, while Southampton were soon to exact their own revenge with a league double over Palace, including a 4-1 defeat at Selhurst Park in the last game of that 1957-58 season, the goals coming from Clifton (2), Reeves - who had scored 35 goals that season - and Paine, while McNichol scored a late consolation goal for Palace. More importantly, of course, this was Palace's last game in the Third Division as they had failed to make the cut in the Southern Section and had been consigned to the newly-formed Fourth Division.

One of Eight New Faces at the Dell

Saints' first season in the new Third Division (1958-59) had proved something of a disappointment as they finished in the bottom half after a good start - and Ted Bates took swift action. When Bernard Harrison joined at the start of 1959-60 he was one of eight new signings, among them players who were crucial to this promotion season, including the new wing-half pairing - creator and destroyer respectively - Dick Connor and Cliff Huxford, and the goal-scoring inside forward George O'Brien. Meanwhile 14 players were released including a disgruntled Don Roper.

Introducing our new players to our Supporters

By courtesy of the Southern Evening Echo.

They are left to right:-

Kennedy, (Pat)   Huxford, (Cliff)   Penzer, (Eddie)   Conner, (Dick)   Wilson, (Keith)
Davies, (Ted)   Womack, (Tim)   O'Brien, (George)

Saints introduce their new players. Bernard Harrison missing as he was still playing cricket.

68

Back from cricket in time for the pre-season trial match, Bernard impressed at outside-right, but it was clear from the outset that he was being earmarked as Terry Paine's understudy. He was contracted to receive a basic £15 per week plus an additional £2 to £5 per week when in the first team, a bonus he was not given the opportunity to collect very often.

SATURDAY, AUGUST 15th, 1959.
ANNUAL CHARITY TRIAL MATCH
(Kick-off 3.00 p.m.)

STRIPES 3.

GODFREY

DAVIES R. 2   TRAYNOR KENNEDY. 3

CONNER 4   PAGE 5   HUXFORD 6

PAINE 7   O'BRIEN 8   REEVES 9   MULGREW 10   SYDENHAM 11

Referee
Mr. H. G. NEW
of Havant

Linesmen
Mr. J. Parry
(Red Flag)
Mr. A. S. Taylor
(Yellow Flag)

WOMACK 11   MURRAY 2 10   MAUGHAN 9   WILSON 8   HARRISON 7

SIMPSON 6   HOLMES   CLIFTON 4

KENNEDY 3 McLean   HEANEY 2

DAVIES E.
WHITES 2.

Saints' Promotion-winning Team

What looks with hindsight a misguided career move by Bernard was perhaps not quite so obviously so at the time. Ted Bates intimated that he wanted Bernard for the first team and not merely as cover for Paine and Sydenham. Terry Paine had by now made the number 7 shirt his own, but John Sydenham had not quite cemented his place on the left. In 1958-59 he had alternated with John Hoskins. In the event Paine did not miss a match in 1959-60, while Sydenham missed only one, and Bernard was restricted to three league appearances, one when Paine switched to the left and twice with Paine at inside-right. Nowadays players miss matches for the slightest niggle but the remarkable stability of that side - Huxford, Connor, O'Brien, and defenders Page, Traynor and Davies were also virtually ever-present during the season - indicates the extent to which players tended, in the days before the introduction of substitutes, to play through injuries. You had to keep playing or the way back might remain closed. Bernard was not the only good player who could not prise his way regularly into this settled side, the others including Terry Simpson at wing-half, Pat Kennedy at full-back, Brian Clifton at inside-forward and Tony Godfrey in goal.

Back row (left to right): D.Scurr, B.Clifton, C.Holmes, T.Mulgrew, B.Harrison. Middle row: W.Maughan, P.Kennedy, D.Conner, R.Reynolds, J.Page, G.Brown, T.Traynor. Front row: J.Gallagher (trainer), J.Sydenham, T.Paine, C.Huxford, G.O'Brien, D.Reeves, E.Bates (manager).

Tony Godfrey reckons it was a case of *"wrong place, wrong time"* for Bernard: *"I played a few games with him for the Reserves and I saw him play in the League side and he always played well. He had a lot of ability and could beat players. If he had a weakness it was perhaps when he had a full-back who was trying to kick him into the stand, not uncommon in those days. But he didn't stand a chance of a regular place because Terry Paine was a fixture whatever form he was in and you had John Sydenham coming through."*

Even so things could still have broken in Bernard's favour in the longer term because, unbeknown to him, both Paine and Sydenham were due for National Service the following season. But when the time came Paine managed by devious means to avoid the call and in the meantime Harry Penk was signed as cover for Sydenham. Bernard's cricket was another factor which counted against him being seriously in contention. Tony Godfrey again: *" I don't think that they really liked relying on players who had the two sports - they often missed pre-season training and later wanted to leave before the end of the season."*

Life at the Dell

In reality things never quite gelled for Bernard at the Dell. Tony Godfrey feels *"he was in some ways his own worst enemy."* From the outset he perhaps created the wrong impression by sometimes arriving late for training, his team-mates having done a few laps of the track as he finally emerged from the tunnel. This made him very popular with his team-mates but went down rather less well with the training staff. In fact this resulted from his dependence on an unreliable train service from Andover rather than from a cavalier attitude. Bernard has never been a car driver and this in itself has probably had an effect on his career decisions. Brother Clive says : "*he became very adept at getting lifts, convincing unsuspecting playing colleagues or opponents alike that Andover was directly on their route home, even if they planned to travel in a completely different direction!".*

But it is true that he found the training sessions uninspiring. He could also be argumentative. He was at constant loggerheads with the reserve team trainer George Horsfall. Horsfall was a typical hard-nosed former full-back and the waif-like Bernard did not quite measure up to his image of a professional footballer. He thought it was his job to toughen players up and would never accept it when a player said he was injured. Tony Godfrey

Who's Who at the Dell

No. 8

BERNARD HARRISON

ALTHOUGH the Saints' Reserves have been having a rather thin time in the Combination League this season, Bernard, who has not missed a match, has shown consistently good form at outside-right.

Fast and elusive, he has continually worried opposing defences and thoroughly justified his selection on Wednesday for the League team for the first time at Barnsley.

Born at Worcester just over 25 years ago, Bernard, son of a schoolmaster and former Mayor of Andover, was an outstanding athlete at Peter Symond's School, Winchester, and was an amateur on Pompey's books before turning professional and joining Crystal Palace.

In just over two seasons with the London club he played in 78 League matches and scored 12 goals. His transfer this summer was a happy move, for as a Hampshire cricketer he has many friends in the county. A useful right-handed batsman and medium pace bowler, he is also a keen golfer and badminton and table tennis player. Was married in August.

recalls: *"I remember him reducing poor Bob Charles to tears as a 17 year-old goal-keeper by continually blasting a heavy ball at him from only a few yards in order to toughen him up".* In Bernard's case he thought that he did not train hard enough, while Bernard always insisted that he was naturally fit and did not need to train as much as some of the others. Only Terry Paine could have argued this with impunity. Indeed he often had a convenient niggle which persisted all week, only mysteriously to recover by match day!

The reserve team squad trained separately from the first team. Sessions invariably began with four laps around the track always led by four players who were George's favourites. They should remain nameless other than for the indecorous nicknames given to them by the others who were less dedicated trainers - "shit, shovel, bucket and spade!". When he chose, Bernard ran the others into the ground just to prove a point. He also boasted to his disbelieving team-mates that he could outsprint John Sydenham - almost an Olympic standard sprinter and six years younger. In the event he ran him very close when a race was arranged.

Overall the team spirit in the squad compared very unfavourably with that he had experienced at Palace, with particular suspicion caused by the influence exercised by Terry Paine who seemed to have a direct line to the Manager over the head of the captain Cliff Huxford. Bernard was on the wrong end of this towards the end of the season when he was amazed to be told by Terry rather than Ted Bates that he was on the transfer list. He nevertheless had a very high regard for Paine as a player - his ability to chip a ball with supreme accuracy with both feet he thinks was quite unsurpassed - and he got on very well with him, possibly because they were both educated at schools in Winchester. Paine was later to join him in a few a cricket matches, often appearing for Bernard's X1.

The Football Combination

It may have appeared to some that Saints simply provided a convenient base for Bernard close to his cricket, but he desperately wanted and needed first team football. Not that life was uninteresting in the Reserves. Saints had finished in third place in Division 2 of the Combination League and had been promoted to Division One, so there were encounters to come with the reserve sides of the top teams in London, including Spurs, Arsenal, Chelsea and West Ham United.

The first match was a tough baptism, Saints losing 4-0 to Tottenham Hotspur's second string at White Hart Lane in August 1959, a team captained by Tony Marchi - who had just re-joined Spurs after two years with Juventus in Italy - and including young Frank Saul, later a Southampton player. One of the goals came from left-winger Terry Dyson, like Marchi a member of Spurs famous Double-winning side of the following season. Saints took time to settle in such company and lost four of the first five matches but then thrashed the West Ham reserve team 5-1. And what a team! The Hammers' line-up that day makes very interesting reading in the light of subsequent events, featuring youngsters Bobby Moore and Geoff Hurst (in his early days at left-half) and the future manager John Lyall. But time and again, the *Echo* reporter noted, Bernard Harrison outpaced the West Ham defence and laid on chances.

One of the early defeats was watched by Ted Bates - unfortunately a poor performance in losing 4-0 at home to Leicester City who included Frank McClintock and Ken Keyworth, players who were to make the Cup Final side beaten by Spurs the following season. "Nomad" in the *Echo* excluded Bernard from his general criticism of the team and Bates would have noted some good approach play by him - in particular one 50 yard burst down the wing which excited the crowd and ended with a cross almost turned in by Scurr.

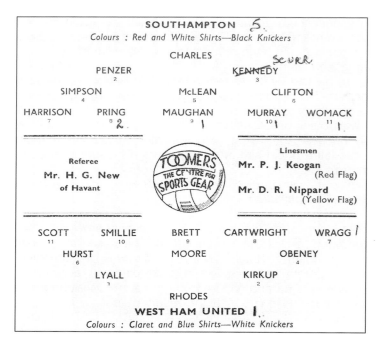

Then Saints Reserves lost at Stamford Bridge to a Chelsea side with two future England internationals in centre-forward Barry Bridges and left-winger Bobby Tambling, and John Sillett - the former Southampton amateur and brother of the more famous Peter - at full-back. Bernard played well enough to attract some interest from the Chelsea manager John Harris. Encouraging rumours of such interest were to persist all season.

League Debut for Saints

Following a number of lively performances Bernard finally got his first team chance when Sydenham dropped out for the match at Barnsley in October 1959. He played with George O'Brien as his inside partner, while Terry Paine switched wings. Despite playing against ten men for most of the game and having most of the play, Saints - in a poor run of form at this stage of the season - could not provide the telling finish and went down to a disappointing defeat by one goal to nil.

Ted Bates frequently suffered interference on playing matters from Directors and on the train journey back from Barnsley Bernard overheard one Board member advise Bates not to pick Harrison again "because he doesn't tackle". The advice was ignored at the time since he was picked for the next match but this attitude may well explain the eventual arrival of Harry Penk who was a relatively 'safe' option, a winger who was unexceptional on the ball but who tracked back more effectively than Bernard - or indeed Sydenham - once possession was lost.

Southampton v. Swindon, 10 October 1959 - Football League Division Three

For the next match Sydenham returned but Bernard retained his right-wing spot as Paine moved to take over from the injured O'Brien at inside-right. Saints returned to form with a crushing 5-1 win to take eighth place in the league. Derek Reeves was a remarkably inconsistent player and as likely to miskick as to score when presented with a chance. But he had an instinct for goal and when it was his day he was devastating. And this was his day as he helped himself to four goals, the third time in the season thus far that he had scored three or more in a match. In so doing became the leading goal-scorer in all Divisions with 19 goals up to that point. He was to go on to create a club record with 39 in League and Cup in the season. The *Southern Evening Echo* very much approved of the new Saints formation:

"Terry Paine made a success of his new position of inside-right. With Bernard Harrison doing well on the right wing the new set-up in the Saints forward line might solve some problems."

Result **Southampton 5** (Reeves 4, Paine) **Swindon 1** Attendance 15,487
Southampton Charles; Davies, Traynor; Conner, Page, Huxford; Harrison, Paine, Reeves, Mulgrew, Sydenham.
Swindon Town Burton; Chamberlain, Bingley; Morgan, Mellor, Woodruff; Corbett, Edwards, Layne, Gauld, Darcy.

Southampton v. Barnsley, 14 October 1959 - Football League Division Three

An unchanged Saints side played the return match with Barnsley on the following Wednesday evening and secured two more points after conceding the lead in the first half. Derek Reeves on this occasion missed a couple of chances and it was left to Tommy Mulgrew to seal the game in the second half, his second and winning goal being placed on a plate for him by Bernard who had another good game on the wing.

<u>Result</u> **Southampton 2** (Mulgrew 2) **Barnsley 1** Attendance 16,937
Southampton Charles; Davies, Traynor; Conner, Page, Huxford; Harrison, Paine, Reeves, Mulgrew, Sydenham.
Barnsley Leeson; Walters, Swift; Bartlett, Hopkins, Barber; Mulligan, Baxter, Stainsby, Beaumont, Lunn.

Bernard then travelled with the team to York only to be left out half an hour before the kick off, and this happened again at Accrington two weeks later when Paine was in doubt. The only other occasion when he looked set to play - but in the end watched from the stands - was an FA Cup Fourth Round replay at Watford in February 1960 which Saints lost 1-0. The crowd for that match was 28,000 and in the previous round a Maine Road crowd of 42,000 had seen them beat Manchester City 5-1, one of Derek Reeves incredible 'on' days when he scored another four.

While Saints' League side went on to clinch promotion as Champions of Division Three, winning by two points from Norwich City, the young Reserve side - stiffened by more experienced players like Bernard (who made 30 appearances), Maughan and Simpson - battled on creditably to safety in the lower reaches of the Combination League Division One. One achievement was to win (2-1) the return match with Spurs Reserves who, as well as Terry Dyson and Tony Marchi, this time also fielded internationals Terry Medwin and Mel Hopkins.

When Terry Paine told Bernard of his release he was shocked but not overly concerned and he went back to cricket with Hampshire in the expectation that a deal might be struck with Chelsea. Rumours of Chelsea's interest had now been confirmed by Ted Bates. However when nothing had materialised by the end of June, when his contract expired, he found himself back in the Fourth Division with a move to Exeter City. It was an unhappy start with his new employers when they refused him the chance to play some Championship cricket games for Hampshire in August.

Southampton Football and Athletic Co., Ltd.

Secretary :
H. F. DIDHAM

Team Manager :
E. T. BATES

Founded 1885

Ground and Registered Office :

THE DELL,
MILTON ROAD,
SOUTHAMPTON.
Telephone 23408

28 APR 1960

Dear Bernard

    In accordance with F. A. Rule 26, we have to advise you that we do not propose to retain your services for the 1960/61 Season, and we have therefore, included your name in our Open-to- Transfer list at a fee of £1,000

    May we take this opportunity of thanking you for your good services, and if we can assist in securing your transfer to another Club, we shall be very happy to do so.

Yours sincerely,

Secretary.

Bernard's Letter of release from Saints

76

CHAPTER FIVE

EXETER CITY .... and Points West

Exeter City was another club who had missed the cut in the old Third Division, finishing way down in 24th place in the Southern Section. They had pushed hard for promotion in their first season in the Fourth Division under the very effective stewardship of the former England international Frank Broome, but had eventually fallen back to finish in 5th place and then 9th the following season of 1959-60. Broome left to manage Southend United and Glen Wilson - a long-serving wing-half with Brighton - was appointed player-manager at the cost of a £5,000 transfer fee.

Exeter were experiencing financial problems and had re-structured their playing staff to such an extent that they had the smallest retained list in the whole of the Football League. It was Wilson, who had played alongside Bernard in the Division Three South representative side, who now signed him from Southampton for £1,000 at the beginning of an unhappy period in charge at St James Park Exeter. Other new signings included Peter Gordon, an inside-forward from Watford (and previously Norwich City), Alan Grant from Brighton, and Alvan Williams from Bradford Park Avenue, of whom only Gordon was to make more than a handful of appearances for the club. One of the players who had been retained was the hard-tackling right-back Theo Foley, who was to win nine caps for Eire and later was a successful coach with Arsenal. They all (except Wilson himself as he missed the early season matches through injury) lined up in the public practice match in August 1960 - when Bernard should have been playing cricket for Hampshire - with Bernard in the likely first team (the 'Reds') who won 5-0, with three headed goals from Jack Wilkinson. Of the newcomers the local press thought that "Harrison and Gordon were the pick of the bunch":

"Harrison is a speed man who knows what to do with the ball when he has made his run and Gordon seems to have all the attributes of an inside-forward".

It was to prove an unhappy stay for Bernard, however, and one which left him disenchanted with professional football. Initially things looked promising enough as he teamed up once more with the highly skilful Gordon Dale, the former Portsmouth left-winger who had been City's most expensive purchase at £7,000 in 1957. With wingers like Harrison and Dale the Exeter faithful had every prospect of very exciting attacking football.

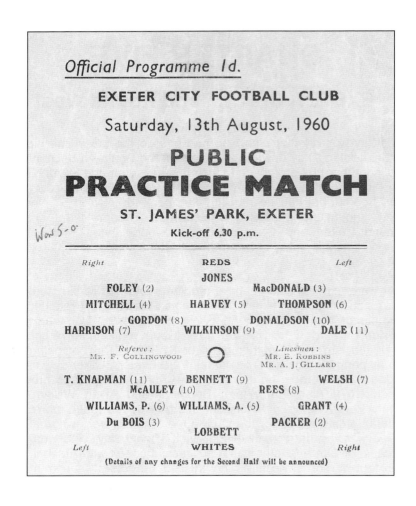

Official Programme 1d.

EXETER CITY FOOTBALL CLUB

Saturday, 13th August, 1960

PUBLIC
PRACTICE MATCH

ST. JAMES' PARK, EXETER

Kick-off 6.30 p.m.

Won 5-0

Right	REDS	Left
	JONES	
FOLEY (2)		MacDONALD (3)
MITCHELL (4)	HARVEY (5)	THOMPSON (6)
GORDON (8)		DONALDSON (10)
HARRISON (7)	WILKINSON (9)	DALE (11)

Referee:		*Linesmen:*
MR. F. COLLINGWOOD	O	MR. E. ROBBINS
		MR. A. J. GILLARD

T. KNAPMAN (11)	BENNETT (9)	WELSH (7)
McAULEY (10)		REES (8)
WILLIAMS, P. (6)	WILLIAMS, A. (5)	GRANT (4)
Du BOIS (3)		PACKER (2)
	LOBBETT	

| Left | WHITES | Right |

(Details of any changes for the Second Half will be announced)

In the first home league match Bernard and Peter Gordon were unveiled as new signings to a crowd just short of 10,000 people, but the game ended in a disappointing 0-0 draw with Carlisle United. The gate dwindled to just over 6,000 for the next home match after two away defeats, both by three goals to one at Wrexham and Rochdale, but Exeter at last registered their first win, albeit only 1-0 over Wrexham with the goal set up by Bernard for Graham Rees. Gordon Dale was sometimes the target of criticism from an impatient home crowd who thought he over-elaborated, but he and Bernard delivered some dangerous crosses. The problem was that the chances they were creating were too often spurned.

George Smith would have been interested had he read the newspaper report:

78

"Harrison is one of the hardest-working wingers that City have ever had, and when he's finished his run he doesn't stand there satisfied - he comes right back to help the defence".

With hindsight one additional point of interest is the appearance of eighteen year-old Wyn Davies, the future Wales centre-forward, who made a goal-scoring debut for Wrexham in the first match and held his place for the return - Maurice Golesworthy in his programme notes making the prophetic assessment that "Wrexham seem to have made a good discovery".

Exeter's second win of the season was a 2-0 defeat of Doncaster Rovers with Harrison and Gordon scoring the goals, but, when they lined up to play Peterborough United at home in late September, City still only had those two victories to their credit in the first ten league matches. Their main problem remained one of scoring goals, having netted only eight.

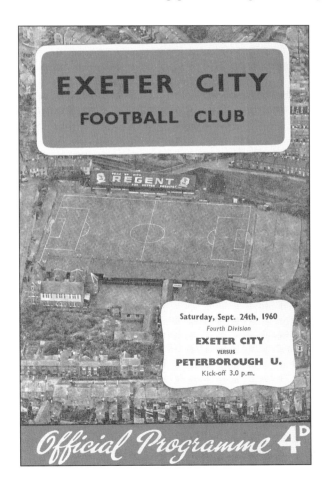

Exeter City v. Peterborough United, 24 September 1960 - Football League Division Four

By contrast, Peterborough United were record goal-scorers - 134 that season - and were en route to the Fourth Division Championship in their first season since winning election to the league. They had been knocking on the door for many years, winning the Midland League five seasons in succession and also carving out a remarkable record as giant-killers in the FA Cup, the best of any non-league club since the war. And in the close season they had also acquired centre-forward Terry Bly from Norwich City, himself renowned in the annals of FA Cup history for his goal-scoring exploits in Norwich City's cup run in 1958-59.

In their non-league days the 'Posh' had commanded better gates than most Third Division sides. Now, in a season when generally gates at football matches were falling alarmingly, they were helping to beat records for crowds in the Fourth Division. Earlier in September they had beaten their closest rivals Crystal Palace 2-0 at Selhurst Park watched by an incredible 36,478 crowd and then had won the return 4-1 before a crowd of over 21,000. Crystal Palace were to set another new record later in the season when 37,774 saw them defeat Millwall.

The visit of Peterborough to St James Park at least saw Exeter score three goals for the first time but the result still ran to form because they conceded four.

Result **Exeter City 3** (Wilkinson 2, Wilson) **Peterborough United 4**
Attendance 9,146
Exeter City Lobbett; Whitnall, MacDonald; Wilson, Harvey, Thompson; Rees, Donaldson, Wilkinson, Gordon, Harrison.
Peterborough United Walls; Stafford, Walker; Raynor, Rigby, Ripley; Hails, Emery, Bly, Smith, Sheavills.

Bernard's Wings are Clipped

Soon things started to go wrong for Bernard personally as well as for the team. Glen Williams was another Manager who wanted to curtail Bernard's dribbling style. Williams at right-half, feeding Bernard on the wing, would despair of ever receiving a return ball. Bernard always wanted to take on and beat his full-back, race deep into the opposition territory to the by-line and cross - the most telling ball in football. This was the way he had played ever since his schooldays and the way in which he had set up so many goals over the years. He was not likely to change now. He admits that he was an "amateur playing a professional game" but it did not suit most coaches and managers who, when under pressure, tended to react negatively, to think first about defending, denying the space that opponents could exploit. Only Cyril Spiers had truly given Bernard scope to express himself and ironically he was to take over briefly at Exeter at the end of the following season after Glen Williams was sacked. But too late for Bernard.

He suffered with an achilles problem and had to miss one or two games but Williams started to use this an excuse to leave him out - often at the last minute - even when he declared himself fit after a week on the treatment table, preferring instead to play young Eric Welsh who was more likely to tow the line. Bernard was particularly upset to miss out on the League Cup tie with Manchester United when he declared himself fit and was desperate to play. His name appears in the programme for the first match , a very creditable 1-1 draw at home, but Williams left him out minutes before the match, insisting that he was not fit. He also missed the replay at Old Trafford when Manchester United re-asserted their superiority with a 4-1 win.

Bernard then played a few reserve team games and proved his fitness but it took an intervention at Boardroom level to secure his last minute recall for a match the day after Boxing Day at Selhurst Park against his old team-mates, a match which was to prove his last in the Football League.

Crystal Palace v. Exeter City, 27 December 1960 - Football League Division Four

Palace had beaten Exeter 3-2 the day before and were riding high in the Division while Exeter were languishing at the very bottom. The Londoners were to win promotion, finishing second to Peterborough both in league position and in goals scored (110) in the season, while City would recover slightly but still have to seek re-election. Palace were now managed by Arthur Rowe, and Johnny Byrne - who was to score 30 in the campaign - was the star player, already an England under-23 international and to go on the full England tour at the end of the season. A number of Bernard's other former team-mates remained too, including Vic Rouse in goal and defenders Johnny McNichol, Alfie Noakes, Gwyn Evans and Terry Long.

A remarkable holiday crowd of 28,551 saw City hang on to a precious point in muddy conditions which were very familiar to Bernard from his days at Selhurst Park, a very good performance in view of the fact that Theo Foley was injured and - in the days before substitutes - limped for the rest of the match on the right-wing. Bernard was playing his third game in four days having played two Reserve games, with Christmas celebrations sandwiched between! The local reporter *Exonian* feared that the pitch would sap the energy of the "frail-looking Harrison" but he underestimated Bernard's strength as he put in a performance which laid to rest any lingering doubts about his fitness. The assessment was that Bernard was not outstanding but that his tricky play had troubled the Palace defence.

Result **Crystal Palace 0 Exeter City 0** Attendance 28,551
Crystal Palace Rouse; McNichol, Noakes; Long, Evans, Petchey; Gavin, Summersby, Uphill, Byrne, Heckman.
Exeter City Jones; Foley, McDonald; Wilson, Harvey, Thompson; Donaldson, Rees, Jenkins, Carter, Harrison.

He was to appear at Selhurst Park one final time in March 1961 in a testimonial match for Roy Greenwood, lining up in an ex-Crystal Palace X1 with former team-mates like Jimmy Belcher, Barry Pierce, and Ray Potter. Mike Deakin had to withdraw with an injury, while Johnny Byrne was away on international duty. The ill-fated Ron Brett of West Ham United played on the left-wing - he was to be killed in a car accident the following year shortly after rejoining Palace.

The Southern League : Poole Town

The narrow-minded enclave that was professional football had by now eroded even Bernard's boyish enthusiasm for the game. He was now a family man with a baby daughter Kim, and twin girls Janet and Susan were to arrive the following year. Susan is now married to Alan Mackrill and their sons Evan and Matthew are already showing early sings of sporting talent in the genes! But back in 1961 Bernard was having look beyond his career in league football at a time when his best years should have been ahead of him. He had decided to take up teaching at Northcliffe private school near Southampton, so responded to the various enquiries he had from non-league clubs over the summer by taking up an offer from Ray King to join Poole Town as a part-time professional on £9 per week for the 1961-62 season. In those days many professionals, in stepping down from the Football League, nevertheless needed to continue to eke out a living from the game and the Southern League provided such opportunities in a good standard of football. Poole Town was a progressive Southern League club who a few years earlier had even attracted the legendary 'Golden Boy' Wilf Mannion to their ranks for a short period. Len Phillips of Portsmouth and England had been another prestigious signing in 1956. Indeed they benefited from the proximity of Portsmouth and to a lesser extent Southampton in their quest for quality players at the end of their careers. The first team squad when Bernard joined was made up almost entirely of former league professionals. Of these full-backs Tommy McGhee and Stan Earl, goalkeeper Fred Brown, and wing-half Ken Ames had all played for Pompey amongst other clubs. Spells with Southampton figured in the experience of forwards Peter Brown and Dennis Pring, while winger Roy Littlejohn - an England amateur international - and wing-half Ted Penzer had both played for Saints Reserves at the same time as Bernard. Of the others centre-forward Jimmy Dailey was a Scot who played over 300 matches for various Football League clubs, while Tom Humphrey played a few games for Aldershot on the wing. Alex Moyse (Bernard's brother-in-law), ex-Crystal Palace, Swindon and Millwall, also had a spell with Poole at this time.

Indeed it took Bernard a few matches with the Reserves in the Western League to get into the side. He was not training with the squad and relied on his natural fitness in playing 20 first team games in what was a Championship-winning season for Poole who just pipped their biggest rivals Wisbech for the title. When they met towards the end of the season it was virtually the Championship decider because Poole were just two points adrift of the leaders Wisbech with a game in hand.

Poole Town v. Wisbech, March 31 1962 Southern League Division One

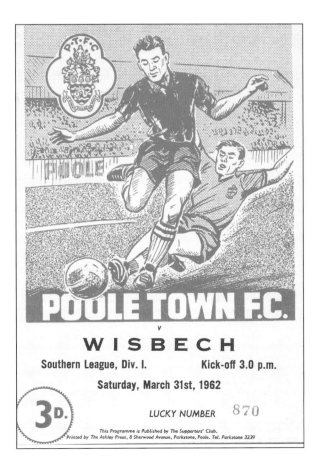

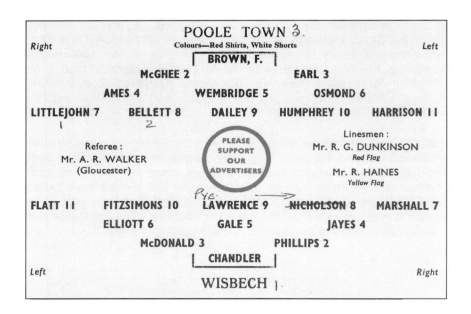

POOLE TOWN 3.

Colours—Red Shirts, White Shorts

Right   *Left*

BROWN, F.

McGHEE 2   EARL 3

AMES 4   WEMBRIDGE 5   OSMOND 6

LITTLEJOHN 7   BELLETT 8   DAILEY 9   HUMPHREY 10   HARRISON 11

Referee :
Mr. A. R. WALKER
(Gloucester)

PLEASE
SUPPORT
OUR
ADVERTISERS

Linesmen :
Mr. R. G. DUNKINSON
Red Flag

Mr. R. HAINES
Yellow Flag

FLATT 11   FITZSIMONS 10   LAWRENCE 9   NICHOLSON 8   MARSHALL 7

ELLIOTT 6   GALE 5   JAYES 4

McDONALD 3   PHILLIPS 2

CHANDLER

Left   *Right*

WISBECH 1.

Wisbech were managed by Jesse Pye, former Wolves and England inside-forward and they had three former internationals in their ranks, notably Billy Elliot - now in his early forties - who played for Sunderland and was capped five times by England at outside-left. The others were only in their early thirties - the left-back Joe McDonald, formerly of Nottingham Forest, Sunderland and Scotland, and inside-forward Arthur Fitzsimmons, ex-Middlesborough and winner of 26 caps for Eire. The winger Terry Marshall had played for Newcastle United.

Poole proved the stronger on the day, winning 3-1 with a goal from Littlejohn and two from leading scorer Peter Bellett who came from the Isle of Wight and was one of the few players in the Poole side lacking Football League experience. This put Poole level on points with a game in hand and proved the platform for them to go on to clinch the Southern League Division One title.

The Western League : Dorchester Town

Marcel Gaillard, the former Portsmouth player who was manager of Dorchester Town, signed Bernard for the 1962-63 season. There he joined a number of former Saints players once again and had the experience playing out wide with Don Roper at wing-half. Roper, an England B international, played nearly 300 games for Arsenal and 120 for Saints and, now aged 40 and with his last club, he was still a strong player capable of explosive shooting. Other ex-Southampton players included Peter Brown once more and full-back Barry Hillier who also played cricket for Hampshire 2nd X1. At the very end of the season Bernard and Hillier both transferred to Andover for one match to help their Hampshire League Division One team avoid relegation. Andover packed their side with players from their Western League team, plus the two new signings, and managed a two-goal victory at Waterlooville to preserve their status.

A Change of Direction with Portals

At this point he was offered the chance to teach Mathematics and to run the cricket and badminton at Millfield School which after much soul searching he turned down in favour of a local position at Portals, a blue-chip company with security paper-making mills at Overton and Laverstoke in Hampshire. His official title of Safety, Security and Personnel Officer masked his true role which was to build up the firm's sports facilities and to produce teams which could compete with those of the giants in the industry such as de la Rue. Much prestige - and no little cash - rested on the annual cricket match with de la Rue and Bernard was expected to deliver his usual century to order. In many ways, although largely consigned to club cricket, he was now at his peak as a cricketer and typically for his new employers each season scored 1,500 runs averaging around 70 and took 70 odd wickets at cheap cost.

Portals owned Laverstoke Park, a very prestigious country estate in the Test Valley, and Bernard was able to oversee the building of a sports and social clubhouse, tennis courts and bowling greens and the development of the superb cricket ground to a standard so that they were able to host Hampshire 2nd X1 and benefit matches. At various stages he was able to offer jobs as groundsmen (and cricketers) to former Hampshire players Lew Harfield, Mervyn Burden and John Newman. He also played for and developed the Company's football team, based on young local players, and took them to cup success and progress from the local junior league into the Hampshire League.

PORTALS AND HAMPSHIRE TEAMS for Peter Sainsbury's Benefit Match

Back Row Lew Harfield, Charlie Smith, Ian McCann, Not Known, Terry Walker, 'Echo' Smith, Michael Williams, Peter Evans, Bill Smith, Peter Lewis, Denis Wiltshire, Not known, Ossie Gooding, Bernard Harrison, Graham Gibbons, Bill Horne.

Front row Keith Wheatley, Roy Marshall, Bryan Timms, Bob Caple, Alan Castell, Julien Sheffield, Peter Sainsbury, Geoff Keith, Alan Wassell, Henry Horton, Danny Livingstone, Jimmy Gray.

Batting at Portals in Peter Sainsbury's benefit match, the beneficiary in the foreground and Keith Wheatley at short leg

86

CHAPTER SIX

HAMPSHIRE COUNTY CRICKET

Hampshire Club and Ground

After his discharge from the RAF back in October 1955 Bernard had, almost on the same day that he signed for Palace, joined the Hampshire CCC ground staff - having secured his release also from the county of his birth, Worcestershire. He had already played in a trial match against Kent Second X1 and, despite two failures, had been offered a contract which was worth £5 a week, not a generous sum unless you had - like Bernard - an additional source of income. He had an exciting year in prospect - his first season in professional football was to be followed by cricket for Hampshire in the summer of 1956.

ON THE HAMPSHIRE CCC STAFF

And he was joining the County at a promising time, since they finished the 1955 season third in the Championship, their highest-ever position. It is no coincidence that this was the West Indian Roy Marshall's first season after serving his period of residential qualification, since he made almost 1,900 runs and he made them quickly. The infinitely reliable pace attack of Derek Shackleton and Vic Cannings was backed up by young bowlers like Malcolm Heath, fast-medium, and spinners Mervyn Burden and Peter Sainsbury, products of Arthur Holt's coaching - 'Holt's Colts'.

By the time Bernard arrived at the County Ground in Southampton to take his place on the Hampshire ground staff he had already made his league soccer debut and was beginning to make progress on that front. He had avoided the boot cleaning and basic tasks which were the lot of the football apprentice. But it was back to the bottom of the pile in cricket. The pervading atmosphere was very much 'them and us' with the capped professionals maintaining a very separate existence. Malcolm Heath, the very tall fast-medium bowler who had one exceptional season for Hampshire in 1958 (126 wickets at 16.42), was a good friend at this time. When he was awarded his county cap he made a joke of it, touching his cap in mock superiority whenever he was practising in a net adjacent to Bernard.

The daily routine of members of the ground staff was an hour's pitch-rolling, then clearing litter from under the seats if there had been a game the day before, before getting down to net practice. Bernard's contemporaries included Derek Tulk, Ray Flood, and John Newman. In the middle it was predominantly matches for the Club and Ground, sixteen in that first season - a very wet summer -, and for the Second X1, a further seven, and a few for Neville Roger's benefit.

IN BATTING POSE AT
NORTHLANDS ROAD

HAMPSHIRE SECOND X1 at Andover in 1957
Back row Arthur Holt (coach), Alan Wassell, Butch White, Derek Tulk, Brian Robbins, John Newman, Roy Stride
Front row Bernard Harrison, Ray Pitman, Rex Chester, Colin Roper, Ray Flood

Bernard and Ray Pitman going out to bat v. Wiltshire at Andover in 1957 Arthur Holt in background (left). They put on 146 (Bernard 90, Pitman 82)

Net Practice under Arthur Holt

Arthur Holt was a very charming man and an encouraging presence at nets, but his only real advice to Bernard as a coach was not to cut until he had 40 on the board, which left him wondering how he would get there by eliminating his most productive stroke! Emphasis was placed on good fielding and the senior players were quick to stamp on any evidence of sloppiness. On one occasion Derek Shackleton had an admonishing word for Bernard when he took a catch at mid-off from his bowling with one hand, rather too casually for Shack's liking. But Desmond Eagar, a fine close catcher and in his last year as captain, was kindly and supportive to Bernard when he dropped two catches in his first team debut match in 1957, saying that he himself had dropped several before his first was safely pouched.

Derek Shackleton tended to avoid nets - he bowled most of the day in the middle - but Bernard acquired an early respect for his bowling. He faced him in pre-season practice matches in each of his first two

Derek Shackleton

seasons and was out on both occasions (for 0 and 13) in exactly the same way, fencing at late away movement off the seam to be caught at the wicket. Shack had remembered: "Didn't I get you that way last year?" The senior batsmen tended to ensure they were on Shack's side in these games! Shackleton's control of line and length was legendary. His economy rate seemed to matter as much to him as his wicket-taking and was as niggardly as any bowler's in the country. Bernard remembers that, when he did a stint helping out in the scorebox, at the end of each session Shack's shouted enquiry would be the same: "how many?".

The fast bowler 'Butch' White appeared at net practice, however, and he did not hold back. He shook up a few young batsmen with some short-pitched deliveries followed by the perennial advice to "get in line son". But he met his match a couple of seasons later when Danny Livingstone, dynamic left-hander from Antigua on trial for Hampshire, caused a sensation by taking him on in the nets, on one occasion hooking him off his nose out of the net and far into the beyond. Arthur Holt was impressed and Secretary Desmond Eagar quickly decided to take him onto the staff.

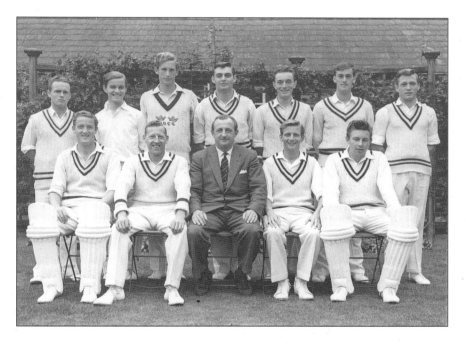

HAMPSHIRE SECOND X1 at Lords in 1961
Back Row - Mike Wells, Peter Wiggins, Charles Fry, John Shippey, Bob Caple, Peter Haslop, Bryan Timms
Front row - Alan Wassell, Mervyn Burden, Arthur Holt, Bernard and Alan Castell

DEREK SHACKLETON'S BENEFIT MATCH at Lyndhurst in July 1958

Back row - Bernard Harrison, Roy Stride, Ray Pitman, Bryan Timms, Colin Roper
Front row - Butch White, Jimmy Gray, Ray Flood, Derek Shackleton, Desmond
Eagar, Mike Barnard

David White was a wholehearted fast bowler to the core. He had a
Trueman-like hatred for anyone with a bat in his hand. A few years later
he agreed to play for Bernard's X1 in a charity match against
Basingstoke but only as a batsman. When he joined Bernard at the
wicket one of the opposing bowlers, with the wicket-keeper standing up,
bowled a beamer which just missed Bernard's head. In the chat at mid-
wicket at the end of the over 'Butch' enquired of Bernard whether it had
been deliberate. When the bowler repeated it in the next over, he had
his answer. Basingstoke then took their turn to bat and when the
offending bowler appeared in the middle to take strike, White could not
be dissuaded from taking the ball. He proceeded to bowl a very
frightening over including a couple of beamers which really shook up the
poor club batsman. He was out two balls later, face as white as a sheet,
and never played for the club again. On another similar occasion
Ingleby-Mackenzie greeted a new batsman with an instruction to 'Butch'
to "give him one" - meaning one off the mark. This had a different
interpretation for White who promptly knocked out all three!

The Footballer/Cricketer

Bernard's sporting life, busy enough at schoolboy level, was now even more hectic. He was asking a lot of himself and there were occasions when he needed to be in two places at once. Inevitably progress in one or both sports was to be affected. Various factors came into play such as coaches in either discipline wondering about his true commitment to their sport; fear of injury affecting his performance towards the end of the football season; and football encroaching into the cricket season leading to disputes between clubs. He missed three Hampshire first team games for which he was selected in August 1960 because his new football club Exeter City would not release him. But Bernard does not regret spreading his talent across the two sports. His regret is not being given a run of consecutive matches in the Hampshire first team. His appearances were dotted throughout six seasons, which did not allow him to work up any consistency nor anyone to judge his true capabilities at county level.

Hampshire's Batting Strength

That his first team appearances were limited to fourteen matches was due to his knocking loudest on the door at precisely the time when the Hampshire batting was at its strongest, with three batsmen - Roy Marshall, Jimmy Gray, and Henry Horton - consistently figuring amongst the top ten or so in the national averages. Moreover they rarely seemed to miss matches through injury. Much in life is about being in the right place at the right time and certainly a number of Hampshire players of similar ability to Bernard, who began their careers either just before or just after this purple patch in Hampshire batsmanship, made many more first team appearances than he did. Peter Haslop, a fast-medium bowler who was a team-mate in the 2nd X1, thinks that *"without doubt he was one of the unluckiest players not to have played regular first-class cricket. Looking back, probably his laid back attitude gave the wrong impression. In fact no one tried more than Bernie. He should have been given a real chance as he was far too good for the 2nd X1, but unfortunately he was put in only when there was an injury to Roy or Jimmy."*

Malcolm Heath agrees that Bernard was a fine player and very unlucky, in both sports: *"It's a question of what might have been - his way was barred by Jimmy Gray in one and by Terry Paine in the other. But he bore his disappointments with great dignity. And it was difficult to get into the Hampshire side then. You had to make a big impact with the very few chances that you got. I myself had Shackleton and Cannings to try and displace!"* But the first team appearances that Bernard did make and the many more in the Second X1, were to give him an experience that he would not have wanted to miss. Peter Haslop again : *"He played on many occasions against real class bowlers who were coming back from injury in the 2nd team. Bernard was always there unruffled, and playing them with all the time in the world."* He was to play against many of the best cricketers of that period - among them Colin Cowdrey, Ted Dexter, John Edrich, Barry Richards and Mike Proctor as youngsters at Gloucestershire, Alan Knott, Derek Underwood, Fred Titmus, Harold Rhodes, and Alan Moss. He was also to encounter famous names from the previous generation of cricketers like England Test players Harold Gimblett (then with Dorset), Maurice Tremlett of Somerset and Jack Robertson of Middlesex. It was usual practice for such players at the end of their careers to captain and coach county second X1s, perhaps batting at 10 or 11. Arthur Holt and Desmond Eagar did so for Hampshire.

And on many occasions in all cricket Bernard was to open with and witness at first hand the scintillating batting of Roy Marshall - most memorably in an opening partnership of 182 against Oxford University in July 1959, to which Bernard contributed just 52. However Roy Marshall was never wholly won over by Bernard's batting: "I had the feeling that he thought I was a little unconvincing outside off stump", an opinion which may also have contributed to his lack of opportunities in the First X1.

Going out to open the batting with Roy Marshall in Vic Cannings Benefit Match in the Parks, Winchester in June 1959. Their century stand took just 28 minutes (Photo: *Hampshire Chronicle*)

Brother Clive thinks he may also have liked the social life a little too much - although he was not alone in that in the Hampshire side. *"Bernie and Derek Tulk used to hit the West End when playing within reach. One day the Seconds were playing Sussex and Hampshire were really struggling against their off-spinner. Bernie was not out overnight, but after a night out with Derek he returned just before the start of play looking decidedly the worse for wear. Arthur Holt was not impressed and said you'd better atone with your performance today. Bernard had had some success with use of pad and some extravagant 'leaves' the day before, but when he left the first ball of the morning he was clean bowled. Arthur Holt, who was doubling as umpire, simply buried his face in his hands in despair."*

Hampshire v the Army - July 1957

Just as National Service threw up some remarkable team sheets in football - the pride of England's future - so it is intriguing to look back at some of the cricketers who appeared in Army teams around this time. Hampshire's annual matches against the Army and the Navy were usually 2-day games and not designated as first-class, but the match against the Army in 1957 was over three days and was a first team match for Hampshire with the Second X1 playing Kent at Gosport. It is open to debate therefore whether this was a first-class fixture. Bernard had played in the equivalent match the year before, his first season, and the Army had included three future England Test players in Harold Rhodes, Phil Sharpe and John Edrich. He had managed to get Sharpe's wicket but had been most impressed by Edrich who "really showed you the maker's name". When Bernard batted he had a frightening experience when Rhodes let go a very quick bouncer which removed his cap, the only protective headgear available in those days. This was the type of delivery which was later to see him no-balled for throwing. Bernard remembers the match also for an extraordinary batting display by the future Hampshire captain Ingleby-Mackenzie - "a really charming man who was much a better batsman than he is often given credit for" - who cut and hooked his way to a whirlwind century in the style of amateurs of old.

Now for the 1957 fixture at Southampton Bernard was joined in the Hampshire team for the first time by his younger brother Clive, on vacation from Oxford University. Clive was a fine all-round games player in his own right and had followed Bernard into both the Hampshire and England Schools cricket teams. The Army once again boasted Sharpe and Edrich in its batting line-up. The match became virtually a two-day affair after rain on the first day and Alan Rayment, captaining Hampshire for the first time, declared behind on the first innings. On the final day the Army set Hampshire a seemingly impossible 188 to win in 98 minutes. Rayment thought the task too steep and, as Clive Harrison had not batted first time around, he gave the brothers the chance to open the innings together. On the way to the wicket the brothers discussed what they thought was expected of them and Clive - a naturally attacking batsman - said "let's go for them". Bernard knew the capabilities of his younger brother. Indeed looking back over a life in cricket he reckons that of the ten best innings that he has ever seen, two were by Clive - but he only admits it in an unguarded moment.

HAMPSHIRE v. THE ARMY
At Southampton July 27, 29 and 30 1957

The Army

A B D Parsons c Roper b White	11	b White	3
P J Sharpe lbw b White	16	c Horton b Sainsbury	15
J H Edrich c Horton b Sainsbury	43	hit wkt b Sainsbury	23
D P T Deshon b Burden	45	lbw b Burden	24
K B Standring c Heath b Burden	15		
*J B Robertson c Roper b Burden	16	not out	24
W M S Withall lbw b Burden	0		
K C Came b Sainsbury	24		
+G Clayton not out	16		
J A Pitt c C Harrison b Sainsbury	17	not out	69
J G Williamson c Rayment b Burden	6		
Extras	3		2
	—		—
TOTAL	212	(4 wkts dec)	160

White 2-31

Burden 5-60

Sainsbury 3-74

White 1-7

Burden 1-43

Sainsbury 2-32

Hampshire

B R S Harrison b Standring	28	not out	60
+C Roper lbw b Williamson	3		
H Horton c Clayton b Pitt	14		
*A W H Rayment c Clayton b Withall	58	c Clayton b Williamson	19
R W C Pitman c Sharpe b Pitt	9	not out	26
B L Reed not out	32	run out	14
M Heath b Withall	0		
P J Sainsbury not out	34		
C Harrison did not bat	----	b Came	66
Extras	9		3
	—		—
TOTAL	(6 wkts dec) 187	(3 wkts)	188

Williamson 1-67

Pitt 2-44

Standring 1-36

Withall 2-18

Williamson 1-53

Came 1-30

Hampshire won by seven wickets

For the task in hand the brothers were perfectly paired - the impetuosity of one and the more measured calculation of the other - and they could have been back under the weeping beech tree at the family Nurseries or on the playing field of Peter Symonds as they put on a remarkable 104 runs in just under the hour. When Clive departed his share was 66 in better than even time, his driving on both sides of the wicket a particularly impressive feature of his innings which included two towering sixes over long-on. When Rayment joined Bernard he caught the mood with four 4s in a nine-minute stay and then Barry Reed was run out with 38 still needed. But, joined by Ray Pitman, Bernard's undefeated innings was perfectly paced and he saw them to an improbable victory with just two minutes to spare.

One of Clive's memories of the game is of being told off for bowling too well! He was still bowling off-spin at this stage and had been brought on simply to feed a declaration. *"When I batted I found that JG Williamson was the quickest bowler I'd faced - and the Northlands road wicket was distinctly quick that day. But my main thought was how do batsmen get out on wickets that are this good? When I got back to the pavilion Harry Altham said that he hoped to see me many times playing for Hampshire."* In the event few opportunities were presented, other than the odd 2nd X1 game.

Second X1 Championship cricket

The 1959 season saw the introduction of the Second X1 Championship - previously all matches had been friendlies except for the Minor Counties championship which had admitted first-class county "2nd X1's in the early fifties - and this brought a more competitive edge to the cricket. Counties were more inclined from then on to field stronger sides. Bernard opened both the batting and the bowling for a strong-looking Hampshire line-up, captained by Desmond Eagar, in the first-ever Championship fixture in May 1959 against Gloucester 2nd X1 - the eventual winners of that inaugural championship competition:
Harrison B. R. S., Flood , Stride, Livingstone, Barnard, Atkins, +Timms, Wassell, *Eagar, White, Robbins. The scores were:
Gloucestershire Second X1 265-5 dec. and 48-6 (White 4-26);
Hampshire Second X1 117 (Barnard 37) and 240 for 8 dec. (Flood 94, Harrison 40, Timms 34 not out). At Southampton May 11 and 12 1959.
<u>Match Drawn</u>

Hampshire 2nd X1 went on to finish 12th of the seventeen counties in that first season of Championship competition in 1959.

Hampshire Second X1 at Havant in 1960
Back row - Roy Stride, Roger Sainsbury, John Shippey, Danny Livingstone, Alan
Castell, David Scurr, Jim Clutterbuck (umpire)
Front - Bernard Harrison, Alan Rayment, Arthur Holt, Ray Flood, Bryan Timms

'Butch' White's four-wicket burst was typical of him, because he could turn a game in a few very hostile deliveries when he got it right. Bernard remembers in one Second X1 game holding on to a spectacular catch in the gulley, White's fourth wicket in four balls. He went on to perform similar feats in first-class cricket, most notably of course a hattrick against Sussex at Portsmouth in 1961 with the first three balls of the last over of the day, followed by a difficult chance dropped by Gray off the fourth and another wicket from the fifth. A bemused Ted Dexter watched from the other end as the last six wickets fell for one run. White added real pace and aggression to the Hampshire attack, taking 124 wickets in 1960, only six fewer than Shackleton, and 117 in 1961.

Hampshire X1 v. FEZELA Touring Side - June 1961

A fixture which takes on an added interest with hindsight was the match in 1961 against the South African touring side, the Fezelas, because they included some of the great names who were to grace the South African Test team which visited England in 1965. They were captained by the Test Match batsman Roy McLean and played 21 matches of which only three were three-day games designated as first-class. They were too strong even for county first teams let alone second X1s,

98

winning the three first-class games with ease, and remaining undefeated on the tour.

Against Hampshire they included in their batting line-up world class players in the making - opener Eddie Barlow and wicket-keeper/batsman Denis Lindsay - and the captain of the 1965 Test side Peter Van der Merwe. More importantly for Bernard Harrison who opened for the Hampshire X1 was the distinctly hostile pace attack of Peter Pollock and James Botten. The Fezelas could have enforced the follow-on but did not and Hampshire just managed to hold on for a draw.

Scores Fezelas 309-7 declared (Burger 78, Gripper 45, McLean 45 not out) and 65-5 declared; Hampshire X1 142 (Bernard Harrison 53) and 163-9 (Gray 53). At Southampton 8 and 9 June, 1961. Match Drawn

Life in the Fast Lane

As an opener it was life in the fast lane - 'Butch' White's belligerence in the nets, Frank Tyson's 25-pace run, glistening toe-cap, 5 slips and all, John Price unfurling his beautiful curving approach, Mike Proctor all swirling arms, bowling off the wrong foot and on you before you realised it, Peter Pollock fast and aggressive, Jack Flavell flame red hair and a quick slingy action. In professional sport, then as now, fear was a constant companion - both fear of being hit and fear of failure. Even Roy Marshall was to admit that no batsmen in those days before protective headgear really liked facing truly quick bowlers. He - bespectacled and almost invariably bareheaded - was potentially more at risk of physical injury than most. His response was one open only to players of genuinely exceptional talent - he simply threw the bat at the ball from the very first delivery and had the ability to succeed in doing it.

Bernard was quick on his feet and had a good eye but he could have been killed when in 1962 he was struck over the eye by a ball from Derbyshire and England bowler Les Jackson, an awkward proposition who cut the ball both ways at fast-medium. It was not unheard of for senior players to miss out on the trip to Derby to face Jackson and Rhodes on what was often a 'green top'. This was such an occasion and Alan Castell recalls with great amusement Bernard's initial response when summoned by Arthur Holt to travel to Derby at short notice: *"Sorry Coach, I can't go because I've no clean kit!"* Indeed Bernard's kit was not often very clean. Travel to Derby he did, however, with painful consequences, but Hampshire - all out for 108 in the first innings, then set 345 to win in 320 minutes - won the match mainly due to one of Ingleby-Mackenzie's greatest innings, an undefeated 111. Derek Shackleton, next man in, did not fancy it and was trying to persuade Bernard to resume his innings. Mercifully, the captain's magnificent effort saw Hampshire home before this was necessary. Bernard was left nursing a 'shiner' which kept him out of the following match against Glamorgan.

After being struck by a lifter from Les Jackson, Bernard shows off his bruise to Hampshire team-mates (from the left) Alan Castell, Geoff Keith, Peter Haslop, and Bob Caple

The controversial Harold Rhodes, another England bowler and later branded a thrower, had a deadly quicker ball and he knocked off Bernard's cap when Hampshire played the Army. But for Bernard the pressure was mental more than physical - never being given a clear run in the team, he was always under pressure to win or to retain a first team spot. As a result he gained a reputation as a grafter, not that he scored particularly slowly but that he had a measured approach and did not throw it away when things were difficult. He was by instinct an accumulator, a conventional opening batsman whose initial job was to take the shine off the ball to allow those who followed to play with more freedom. He was mainly a back foot player, strong on the offside, a good cutter and with an attractive cover drive but not given to big shots. But brother Clive reckons the County coached the flair out of him: *"as a young player he used to play with an open blade, crashing the ball square of cover. But they got him to push drive more through extra-cover and to cut more safely by patting down on top of the ball. They groomed him simply as an opening batsman when he could have played in the middle-order too. His bowling too could have been developed."*

There were times when he shook off his more calculated style and put the bowling to the sword, notably when he scored what the *Southampton Echo* described as "a glorious century" against Middlesex Second X1 at Enfield in 1960 - sixteen fours and a six in making 125 in 189 minutes. In 1962 at Taunton he hit 102 not out against Somerset 2nd X1 in 120 minutes. Once he had been released by Hampshire and he stayed on to play for the Second X1 as an amateur, the pressure had gone and he played more often with this sort of freedom.

But Bernard was more in his element when he had to battle it out against good bowlers. The use of uncovered wickets nurtured skills in coping with the turning ball - facing the likes of David Allen, Fred Titmus and 'Bomber' Wells on a helpful surface with three short-legs picking your pocket -, skills which young batsmen today do not get the chance to develop. He faced Jim Laker and Lance Gibbs only in benefit games but they gave it more rip than anyone he ever encountered. But one of the greatest challenges for batsmen in England over the next few years was facing the left-arm spin of Derek - soon to be 'Deadly' Derek - Underwood, especially on a drying wicket.

Kent Second X1 v. Hampshire Second X1 - May 1962

Bernard remembers his tussle with Underwood as a 17-year old in 1962 in a Kent Second X1 side which was laced with future Test players and was in due course to form the basis of a very successful County team. In the first innings of a match at Beckenham Bernard hit eight boundaries in an enterprising knock of 55 as Hampshire finished on 152, with Underwood taking 5-45 including a spell of 4-15 as the wicket dried out. Even in those early days Underwood really gave the ball a tweak at virtually medium pace. Bernard worked out a way of playing him which was in normal circumstances to play forward to his seamer - which at this stage in his development he betrayed by covering the ball as he ran up - and back to everything else. But in the second innings the Beckenham wicket was even more unpredictable. Underwood was to become virtually unplayable on such a surface - as the Australians were to discover at the Oval six years later. Here young off spinner Michael Olton was equally so (taking 6-5 in 7.2 overs) and they bowled out Hampshire for 48 in under two hours with Bernard, in one of his most skilful knocks, the only player to reach double figures. From there the two young spinners' careers took very different paths - Olton was to make only one first-class appearance for Kent.

Second XI Championship KENT v. HAMPSHIRE
At Beckenham 7, 8 May 1962

Hampshire

B R S Harrison b Luckhurst	55	c Catt b Underwood	19
B S V Timms b Reader	16	b Olton	8
G L Keith c Nicholls b Underwood	49	c Dye b Underwood	1
D O Baldry c Page b Luckhurst	5	b Olton	5
R G Caple c Constant b Olton	1	c Constant b Olton	2
M Green b Underwood	6	c Denness b Underwood	6
P Stevens c Luckhurst b Underwood	0	c Denness b Underwood	2
A Castell not out	2	b Olton	1
P Haslop c Dye b Underwood	0	not out	1
D W White b Underwood	4	st Catt b Olton	0
R Cottam lbw b Olton	2	b Olton	0
Extras	12		3
TOTAL	**152**		**48**

Underwood 5-45   Underwood 4-15
Luckhurst 2-36   Olton 6-5

Kent

B Chivers c Castell b Caple	9	lbw b Caple	1
D Nicholls c Haslop b Keith	31	not out	16
D Constant c Keith b Caple	0	not out	10
M Denness b Keith	3		
B Luckhurst c and B Caple	42		
A W Catt c Green b Cottam	55		
M Olton c Castell b White	13		
D Reader b White	2		
D Underwood not out	7		
J Dye c Cottam b White	0		
J C Page not out	6		
Extras	5		
TOTAL	**(9wkts dec) 174**	**(for 1 wkt)**	**27**

White 3-39 Caple 3-48

Kent won by nine wickets

Various things had conspired to limit Bernard's first team chances but he had been the leading light of Hampshire 2nd X1 for a number of years, and was to average over 40 in four successive seasons - 1959, 1960, 1961 and 1962. Of the batsmen only the spectacular Danny Livingstone had made a more compelling case for promotion and he had already leap-frogged Bernard into the County side on merit.

In the 1961 *Hampshire Club Handbook* Desmond Eagar in his review of the previous season provided the following assessment of Bernard's chances:

"B. R. S. Harrison, who has only played in seven first-class matches, has scored heavily for the Second X1 and Club and Ground for some seasons. He was selected in his own right for a minimum of three county matches in August last year. Unfortunately, as a professional footballer, he had to miss the opportunity offered to him. With tremendous concentration and a good head for games, Harrison could well become a regular member of the side, and he is a most useful close-to-the -wicket fielder."

Meanwhile John Arlott in the *Playfair* Cricket Annual considered that: *"Danny Livingstone and the unlucky Bernard Harrison look the best young batting prospects."*

Batting at Lords v. Middlesex
Second X1, August 1961 - Ernie Clifton
keeping wicket and John Sheppard at slip

1961 was the year of Hampshire's first Championship title and it was make or break year for Bernard. He ran into a spell of form in June which, in most circumstances, would have demanded that he play a bigger role in Hampshire's quest for the title. A score of 48 against Kent 2nd X1 was followed by his 53 against the Test-quality attack of the South African Fezelas. He then took 96 off the Free Foresters for Lord Porchester's X1 followed by 101 and 20 for Hampshire 2nd X1 v. Sussex; on to Henley-on-Thames where he got 101 against Oxfordshire ; then 51 for Roy Marshall's X1 before going back to his home ground, May's

Bounty at Basingstoke, for a first ball duck (playing for non-existent swing because they opened with an old ball!) and an undefeated 113 in 148 minutes in a successful run chase against Somerset 2nd X1. Into July, he made for 57 (run out) and 5 in a three-wicket win over Middlesex Second X1 when, at last, an opportunity presented itself. He was to travel to Birmingham the next day with the first team squad as cover for Roy Marshall who had strained a knee in the win over Essex. Marshall, batting with a runner, had made 36 not out in 44 minutes to help the brilliant Ingleby-Mackenzie (132 not out) to win a thrilling run chase on the last day which was so typical of Hampshire's exciting cricket in the Championship year. Ingleby-Mackenzie, yet again, had induced a declaration from an opposing captain which had led to a Hampshire victory. The Essex captain Trevor Bailey was not given to generosity on a cricket field, but he later admitted that he had not expected Marshall to be able to bat.

Hampshire v. Warwickshire - July 1961

Marshall failed a fitness test at Edgbaston the next morning and had to sit out a Championship match for the first time in six years. Bernard opened the batting with Jimmy Gray whom was brilliantly caught by M. J. K. Smith at short-leg with the score on 14. Now Bernard was joined by Henry Horton, a very staunch competitor and of course a member of the footballer/cricketer fraternity. Horton, who had an extraordinarily ungainly stance but played very straight once the ball was delivered, was a key batsman in the Championship side and was to score over 2000 runs in the season. For Bernard he was also "the nicest and most approachable of the leading capped professionals".

They mounted a relatively modest but important partnership which yielded 63 runs, constructed in testing conditions against an attack including two of the most accurate swing and seam bowlers of the day, Tom Cartwright and Jack Bannister. Hampshire were eventually able to declare at 287-9 with Horton top-scoring with 88, well supported by Peter Sainsbury who had by now matured to genuine all-rounder status, contributing 49. In their turn Warwickshire also batted slowly but purposefully and were able to declare two runs on. But, going in a second time with just two overs left on the second evening, Hampshire lost both Gray and Harrison to Bannister without scoring - the umpire being hoodwinked into giving Bernard out lbw depite his having got a nick, an annoyance at any time but rather more important when your place in the side is at stake. It still rankles with Bernard as he thinks he was "cheated out". This left Horton to mount yet another rearguard action, partnered by the ever-reliable Peter Sainsbury, which allowed Hampshire to set a target on the last day, Warwickshire eventually just running out of time in their pursuit of 177 in 130 minutes.

WARWICKSHIRE v. HAMPSHIRE
At Birmingham July 5, 6, 7 1961

Hampshire

J R Gray c M Smith b Thompson	7	c Fletcher b Bannister	0
B R S Harrison c Ratcliffe b Bridge	26	lbw b Bannister	0
H Horton c Fletcher b Bridge	88	c A Smith b Bannister	52
D A Livingstone hit wkt b Thompson	33	c M Smith b Bannister	18
P J Sainsbury c Fletcher b Bannister	49	c Bannister b Bridge	50
D O Baldry lbw b Thompson	10	c and b Bridge	3
*+ A C D Ingleby-Mackenzie			
b Bannister	11	c Horner b Bannister	14
A Wassell c Fletcher b Bannister	6	lbw b Bridge	0
D Shackleton not out	32	c M Smith b Bridge	6
D W White b Bannister	5	not out	10
M Heath not out	9	c M Smith b Bannister	13
Extras	11	Extras	12
	—		—
TOTAL (9 wkts dec)	287		178

Thompson 3-51	Bannister 6-66
Bannister 4-87	Thompson 0-24
Cartwright 0-54	Cartwright 0-18
Bridge 2-67	Bridge 4-58
Hitchcock 0-17	

Warwickshire

N F Horner c Gray b Heath	12	b Shackleton	41
D P Ratcliffe lbw b Shackleton	10	did not bat	
B E Fletcher c Sainsbury b Gray	18	c Wassell b Shackleton	24
*M J K Smith c Sainsbury b Heath	88	b Heath	12
T W Cartwright not out	84	b Shackleton	1
J M Kennedy c Sainsbury b White	29	not out	22
R E Hitchcock			
c Ingleby-Mackenzie b Shackleton	19	lbw b Heath	38
+A C Smith c Harrison b Heath	17	c Ingleby-Mackenzie	
		b Heath	11
J D Bannister not out	6	c Livingstone b Heath	1
W B Bridge did not bat		not out	0
Extras	6		8
	—		—
TOTAL (7 wkts dec)	289	(7wkts)	158

Shackleton 2-72	Shackleton 3-58
White 1-45	White 0-19
Heath 3-73	Heath 4-73
Gray 1-24	
Wassell 0-36	
Sainsbury 0-33	

Match Drawn

The next fixture was against Oxford University at Portsmouth and this gave Hampshire the opportunity to rest key players and to blood some of the younger ones. In retrospect this looks like a free-for-all fought out between the players on the fringes of the side at a time when competition for places in a winning team was intense. Bernard Harrison had to make the most of his opportunity but, although a natural opening batsman, he knew he would have to drop down the order if he was to retain his place once Marshall returned. In the middle order Danny Livingstone was now well established so the competition was effectively between Bernard, Denis Baldry, and Mike Barnard for the number six slot. Mike Barnard was a fine strokeplayer and slip-field but he had not quite fulfilled his potential and an early loss of form in 1961 had seen him give way to Denis Baldry. Baldry was a bit of a live-wire who, having achieved little with Middlesex, had enjoyed a remarkable purple patch at the start of his Hampshire career in 1959. He had scored 151 on debut, then 123 in his third match, and had already been awarded his county cap when in his fifth he showed his versatility by taking 7-76 against Lancashire. Another century was to follow in a sequence of scores remarkable for a player who was to finish with a career average of just 20.

Hampshire v. Oxford University, July 1961

Leo Harrison - no relation - was returning from injury and he captained the Hampshire team which saw the introduction of Caple, a left-hander and another middle order protagonist, and Alan Castell. Castell was a very promising young leg-spin bowler who later lost confidence through lack of opportunity and whom regretfully was persuaded to become yet another medium pacer. The University included two players who had also played a few matches for Hampshire, Dan Piachaud and Charles Fry, grandson of C. B.

Also included was the Indian Test batsman A. A. Baig who two years before had become Bernard's only first-class victim: his bowling was largely overlooked in the first-class game - "I suppose I wasn't quick enough". Peter Haslop, who can boast Hanif Mohammed as one of his two first-class victims, thinks that Bernard's bowling was very under-rated: *"Bernard would always be trying and doing something with the ball. I remember a game against Middlesex Seconds, Knocker White was batting and he was really getting stuck into me, then Bernie came on and pitched the first ball up, a floating awayer, Knocker gave it everything and got a little edge to the 'keeper. Bernie turned to me with a grin "You have got to do that little bit Hassers".*

Bernard Harrison remained in the confident batting form that had characterised his summer and it was he and Mike Barnard who did most to advance their claims against the University. Responding to Oxford's first innings of 313, Bernard opened the Hampshire innings with wicket-keeper Bryan Timms and evidently impressed John Thicknesse of the *Times* who reported that *" he was off the mark with a delicious late-cut and within a short time had played three others, none of which I have seen equalled this season".* He hit seventeen fours in all and enjoyed good partnerships both with the free-scoring Mike Barnard and with Danny Livingstone. The latter stand included a spell of 46 runs in 11 scoring strokes without changing ends. Baldry just missed out on a half-century. After a difficult journey through the nineties, Bernard reached his first - and as it turned out his only - century in first-class cricket before falling to a stunning caught and bowled by Pithey for 110. Hampshire declared 25 runs ahead and then the University again batted well - Alan Wassell was the most successful bowler, taking six with his slow left-arm spin on what was traditionally a seamers' wicket - and set Hampshire a very challenging target of 234 for victory in 145 minutes. That they achieved it - with just a minute to spare - was largely down to some very enterprising hitting from Danny Livingstone and Leo Harrison.

HAMPSHIRE v. OXFORD UNIVERSITY
At Portsmouth July 8, 10, and 11 1961

Oxford University

D B Pithey c Caple b Heath	3	b Heath	19
D R Worsley run out	2	c Barnard b Heath	18
A A Baig b Baldry	1	c Castell b Wassell	53
D M Green c Timms b Heath	62	c Livingstone b Wassell	49
C A Fry c Castell b Heath	4	c Caple b Wassell	23
F W Neate c Barnard b Heath	112	c and b Wassell	40
C D Dryborough b Baldry	52	c Barnard b Wassell	12
A R Duff lbw b Baldry	3	st L Harrison b Caple	10
J D Piachaud not out	27	st L Harrison b Wassell	1
T R Jakobson c Wassell b Heath	14	not out	17
C Potter c Heath b Castell	26	c Barnard b Caple	13
Extras	7		3
	---		---
TOTAL	313		258

Heath 5-78	Heath 2-32
Baldry 3-56	Wassell 6-86
Castell 1-56	Caple 2-33

Hampshire

B R S Harrison c and b Pithey	110	c Pithey b Potter	15
B S V Timms c and b Potter	2	c Fry b Jakobson	7
H M Barnard b Piachaud	75	c Duff b Potter	19
D A Livingstone c Fry b Pithey	39	c Jakobson b Piachaud	79
D O Baldry lbw b Jakobson	48	b Piachaud	20
R G Caple c Fry b Jakobson	25	c Worsley b Dryborough	2
L Harrison b Jakobson	11	not out	75
A Wassell c Baig b Jakobson	20	did not bat	
A T Castell b Jakobson	0	not out	2
M Heath not out	0	did not bat	
M D Burden did not bat		c and b Dryborough	11
Extras	8	Extras	7
	---		---
TOTAL (9 wkts dec)	338	(7 wkts)	237

Jakobson 5-61	Jakobson 1-54
Potter 1-55	Potter 2-42
Piachaud 1-76	Dryborough 2-62
Pithey 2-29	Piachaud 2-72

Hampshire won by three wickets

Hampshire v. Nottinghamshire - July 1961

It was back to the essential business of the County Championship at Southampton the following day and, in the continuing absence of Roy Marshall, Bernard opened with Jimmy Gray. Gray went with just 8 on the board and Bernard followed with the score on 42 and it took a fine knock from Livingstone (88) for Hampshire to struggle through to 178 all out. But a great spell by 'Butch' White (7-61) restricted Nottinghamshire's lead to 29. And the second time around Gray and Harrison provided a much better base, failing to post a century opening partnership only by four runs as Bernard played on to the off-spin of 'Bomber' Wells for 48, attempting a late cut to reach his half-century. Denis Baldry capitalised on this sound start with a brilliant 61 made in 30 minutes and Hampshire were able to set a target of 196 in 125 minutes. Nottinghamshire looked well set as a stand between wicket-keeper Millman and Maurice Hill put on 112 for the third wicket, but both were out to Wassell. And it was his bowling and the excellent fielding which characterised this Championship-winning side which saw the home county secure the victory with three minutes to spare - the last two wickets falling to direct-hit run outs as the final pair sportingly continued their pursuit of the runs rather than attempting to shut up shop.

Hampshire had bagged another 12 precious points, but Bernard was left to ponder whether he would make the team for the match the following day against Glamorgan at Bournemouth. In the event Marshall returned from injury and Baldry had secured his place for the moment, so Bernard was consigned to a familiar diet of Second X1 and Club and Ground fixtures. Marshall and Gray remained fit and were in tandem for the remainder of the season while in the middle order Mike Barnard in due course ousted Denis Baldry once more and went on to play one or two important knocks in the run-in to the Championship. And despite a poor batting performance and defeat against Glamorgan, Hampshire picked up their winning habit once more and continued on their merry way to clinch their first-ever title. Malcolm Heath recalls that on the day the Championship was won he and Bernie were on the golf course rather than where they wanted to be - participating in this triumph: *"Of one thing you can be sure - Bernie would have won our game of golf!"*.

HAMPSHIRE V. NOTTINGHAMSHIRE
At Southampton July 12, 13, 14 1961

Hampshire

B R S Harrison c Winfield b Corran	16	b Wells		48
J R Gray c Winfield b Davison	2	c Forbes b Morgan		84
H Horton c Davison b Corran	25	b Wells		0
D A Livingstone c Millman b Corran	88	c Hill N. b Wells		4
P J Sainsbury c Forbes b Corran	0	did not bat		
D O Baldry lbw c Millman b Corran	11	not out		61
* A C D Ingleby-Mackenzie				
c Winfield b Corran	4	c Clay b Morgan		18
+L Harrison c Winfield b Wells	23			
A R Wassell lbw b Wells	1			
D Shackleton c Hill N. b Wells	0	not out		5
D W White not out	5	c Bilbie b Morgan		1
Extras	3	Extras		3
TOTAL	178	(6 wkts dec)		224

Corran 6-61   Wells 3-61

Davison 1-72   Morgan 3-104

Wells 3-18

Nottinghamshire

N Hill c Ingleby-Mackenzie b Wassell	26	c Horton b Shackleton		5
H M Winfield lbw b White	20	c Gray b Shackleton		4
+G Millman b Sainsbury	48	c Harrison L. b Wassell		67
M Hill c Horton b White	6	c Baldry b Wassell		46
*J D Clay c Wassell b White	4	c Harrison L b White		4
R Bilbie c Livingstone b White	0	c Harrison B b Wassell		24
C Forbes c Horton b Wassell	21	run out		7
I Davison c Horton b White	52	b White		13
A J Corran not out	21	c Harrison B b Wassell		4
B D Wells c Harrison L b White	2	not out		1
M Morgan b White	0	run out		0
Extras	7	Extras		5
TOTAL	207			180

White 7-61   Shackleton 2-57

Wassell 2-57   White 2-78

Sainsbury 1-15   Wassell 4-40

Hampshire won by 15 runs

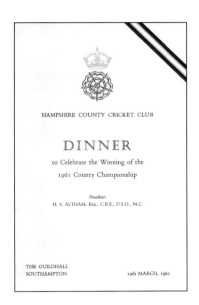

Back row (left to right): A. G. Holt (coach), D. O. Baldry, D. W. White, M. Heath, A. Wassell, D. A. Livingstone, H. M. Barnard, N. Drake (scorer). Front row (left to right): P. J. Sainsbury, M. D. Burden, D. Shackleton, R. E. Marshall, A. C. D. Ingleby-Mackenzie (captain), L. Harrison, J. R. Gray, H. Horton. On ground: B. S. V. Timms, B. R. S. Harrison.

HAMPSHIRE - CHAMPION COUNTY 1961

1961 turned out to be a pivotal season for Bernard. He had run into some of the best form of his career and yet had not been granted a prolonged run in the side. He had averaged 36 for the first-team, 40 for the 2nd X1, and 52 for the Club and Ground, yet had played only a peripheral role in a historic year for Hampshire. But he was a useful member of the squad, perhaps too useful as he had been denied the opportunity to join Nottinghamshire who had made an approach to offer him the prospect of more regular first-class cricket in a 5-year contract.

United Services Officers' Ground · Portsmouth

OFFICIAL CARD 6d

HAMPSHIRE v MIDDLESEX

Wednesday, Thursday and Friday 15th, 16th and 17th August, 1962

HAMPSHIRE	First Innings	Second Innings
1 B. Harrison		
2 J. R. Gray		
3 H. Horton		
4 D. A. Livingstone		
5 P. J. Sainsbury		
6 D. O. Baldry		
*7 A. C. D. Ingleby-Mackenzie		
†8 B. S. V. Timms		
9 D. Shackleton		
10 A. Wassell		
11 M. Burden		

	Extras		Extras

Wkts.	1st 1—	2—	3—	4—	5—	6—	7—	8—	9—
Down	2nd 1—	2—	3—	4—	5—	6—	7—	8—	9—

BOWLING ANALYSIS	—	O	M	R	W	O	M	R	W

MIDDLESEX	First Innings	Second Innings
1 R. A. Gale		
2 W. E. Russell		
3 R. A. White		
4 R. Pearman		
5 E. A. Clark		
6 F. J. Titmus		
7 M. J. Smith		
8 C. D. Drybrough		
9 A. Waite		
*10 A. E. Moss		
†11 M. O. C. Sturt		

	Extras		Extras

Wkts.	1st 1—	2—	3—	4—	5—	6—	7—	8—	9—
Down	2nd 1—	2—	3—	4—	5—	6—	7—	8—	9—

BOWLING ANALYSIS	—	O	M	R	W	O	M	R	W

*Captain   †Wicket Keeper   Umpires— J. Langridge and A. Jepson
Luncheon Interval 1.30 to 2.10   Snack Lunches and Tea may be obtained on the Ground
Hours of Play:
1st day-11.30 to 6.30 p.m.   2nd day-11.30 to 6.30 p.m.   3rd day-11.30 to 6 or 6.30 p.m.
MIDDLESEX WON THE TOSS   Scorers N. Drake and J. Aldis

The 1962 season proved something of an anti-climax for him. While again topping the 2nd X1 averages with 44.07, second team cricket was not an end in itself. Jimmy Gray has pointed out that there are important thresholds in a cricket career which have to be crossed and one of the most critical is to progress from the 2nd X1 into the first class arena. Gray has also reflected that it was so much easier for young players to make that transition in the early years after the war when he was making his way and when Hampshire were of necessity looking to nurture their own local talent. But by the late 1950s the competition for batting places in a more successful side had become intense. Consistent performances in the 2nd X1 constituted the only available platform for promotion to the first team, but by no means guaranteed such elevation. In 1962 Bernard was granted only five first team games. Peter Haslop feels he only needed more of a run in the first team: *"I know he would have got lots of runs, because he would have worked things out, he has got a great cricketing brain. He knew his limitations and he played to them, and he knew the weaknesses of the opposition. There was hardly a Second team game in which he failed, his record speaks for itself."*

He played in three consecutive Championship matches in August against Sussex (twice), and Middlesex and made 3 (c Oakman b Dexter batting at number 6), 10, 34, 1 and 24. In the Middlesex match Bernard opened with Jimmy Gray and, while each was a perfect foil for Marshall, in his absence they were not the ideal pairing for a run chase. Requiring 216 at 84 an hour after Middlesex declared on the last day, they were under instructions to force the pace for victory - but Gray made it clear that slogging was not on his agenda. Both got bogged down against a good quality attack which include the lively pace of Alan Moss and the guile of

Malcolm Heath

Fred Titmus' off-spin. Bernard - the player under pressure for his place - was eventually forced into an uncharacteristic slog off Titmus and was caught for 34.

But decisions about the annual release of playing staff had probably already been taken and Bernard, shortly after being notified of his first rise in pay to £6 a week, was listed - along with his friend Malcolm Heath who had a persistent hip injury - amongst the players jettisoned at the end of the season as the

Club sought to reduce its costs. Bernard, who had already accepted that the methodical team play which increasingly characterised league football could no longer find a place for his outstanding individual talent, now tasted the bitter pill of failure in his other sport. Ironically this was the game in which he himself took a more measured and orthodox approach. Sadly he had effectively dissipated the most important years in his cricket development in pursuit of a chance that never really came. Hampshire had held on to him long enough to nullify his chances of building a career with another county. He was leaving the first class game without really knowing how good a player he was.

John Arlott, a friend of the Harrison family through connections with Basingstoke and North Hants Cricket Club, was so incensed at his release that he threatened to resign his membership of the Hampshire County club. Only ten months earlier Arlott, writing in the *Playfair Cricket Monthly,* had highlighted Bryan Timms and Bernard as two players important to Hampshire's future:

"Bernard Harrison is a grafting batsman who will score more hundreds.....he will take the next batting place and should hold it for years to come."

And with hindsight it does look like bad long-term planning, given the age structure of the Hampshire batting strength at that time. The County now entered a period when the consistency of its batting declined. Jimmy Gray averaged less than 20 in 1963 and from then on was not consistently available. So ironically by the mid-sixties there was no specialist to open the batting with Marshall and first Mike Barnard and then Barry Reed were pressed into the job without great success, while - with Denis Baldry having retired from first class cricket soon after Bernard's release - the middle order became distinctly brittle too.

Leo Harrison, who made such a good job of captaining the Second X1, persuaded Bernard to continue to play for the club as an amateur and he did so periodically until 1968.

Hampshire County Cricket Club

Secretary:
E. D. R. EAGAR

Assistant Secretary:
N. B. EDWARDS

County Cricket Ground

Southampton

Telephone : 24155

10th October,1962.

Ref:PL/W.

To whomsoever this may concern.

B.R.S. Harrison has been a member of our playing staff for a number of years. Unfortunately we are having to dispense with his services as we find ourselves compelled to cut down on our staff. We are very sorry indeed to see him go.

Bernard Harrison is a fine cricketer, who has not had the best of luck since his career has coincided with the two great opening batsmen R.E.Marshall and J.R.Gray. He has played 14 matches for the County and has made one century and two 50s. He has, however, made many thousands of runs for our 2nd XI. and Club and Ground.

Apart from his ability as a cricketer, he is also a fine footballer, having been on the books of the Southampton Football Club and other wellknown clubs.

Apart from his athletic abilities, Bernard Harrison is a most delightful personality who has given very loyal and faithful service to this Club. He is a hard worker at whatsoever he undertakes but my abiding memory of him is his loyalty and honesty.

E.D.R.Eagar.

Secretary.

Testimonial letter from Hampshire CCC secretary Desmond Eagar,
10 October 1962

115

CHAPTER SEVEN

THE CLUB CRICKETER:
BASINGSTOKE & NORTH HANTS CRICKET CLUB

Seven Decades

As a twelve year-old Bernard had often accompanied his father with the Basingstoke and North Hants first X1 in the hope that they might prove to be a player short. When his dream became a reality and he played his first game on August 1st 1947 against Old Redingensions at Reading (scoring ten batting at number 9 and taking two wickets) no one could have imagined that he was to represent the club in seven different decades up to 2000. Even more remarkable is the fact that he is not the only player in the history of the club to have done this, the same feat having been achieved exactly 50 years before.

A Tale of Two Cricketing Families

Still playing occasionally in 1947, his 70th year, was a legendary figure in Basingstoke cricket circles, Bert Butler who in a match with Bournemouth that season incredibly took five wickets in seven balls including a hat-trick. He also complained to the committee that he was not getting enough cricket! He had first played for the club fifty years before in 1897 and had been the groundsman since 1899. Much revered by John Arlott as a boy, 'Old Man' Butler was a right-hand batsman and a slow left-arm bowler of considerable guile who invariably bowled wearing a cap. He played his last match in 1950 to notch up his record of appearances across seven decades and in his career with Basingstoke did the 'Double' (1,000 runs and 100 wickets) three times and scored over 21,000 runs - all without the protection of a box! - and took over 1,800 wickets. Curiously once he had retired as player and May's Bounty groundsman he would never again enter the ground, although occasionally he could be seen watching through the railings.

The Butlers as a family played a pivotal role in Basingstoke's cricket in the first half of the twentieth century, a role which is only rivalled by that of the Harrisons mainly in the latter stages of the century. Bert Butler's three sons - Jim, Fred and Bert junior - all played for the club. Fred was club captain in 1958, a left-hand opening batsman who made over 13,000 runs from 1929 to 1965, good enough to play a number of matches for Hampshire Second X1, and a leg break bowler with a curious action, delivering the ball from behind his ear.

Bert Butler and his three sons

The Harrison family's involvement dates back to 1936 when father Reg played his first match for the club. He was to be elected club captain in 1951 and he led the side from 1951 to 1953, and both sons Bernard and Clive were later to follow him in this role, the former from 1970 to 1981. Clive was a fine striker of the ball - too inclined to take risks early in his innings, though, according to his brother - and a more than useful seam bowler. Bernard - who emulated Bert Butler's record of playing in seven decades with his final appearance in July 2000 against London Bohemians - only played intermittently for the Basingstoke club in the early days because of his County commitments, his football, and his occasional spells with Andover Cricket Club and the longer period with Portals (1963-67). However the all-round accomplishments of the two brothers were a major factor in the success of the club both pre- and post- the advent of competitive league and cup cricket in 1968. Each was to score more than 20,000 runs and take around 1,500 wickets, with Bernard achieving the 'Double' in 1973. All told the Harrisons scored a combined 50,309 runs and took 3,094 wickets and the Butlers 42,314 runs and 2,106 wickets.

In recent seasons another talented family has emerged in Basingstoke cricket, the Nurse family - Leon, still a very good batsman at over 50 years of age, and sons Lee, an opening batsman for Berkshire, and the emerging player young Damien.

Reg Harrison with sons Bernard and Clive at May's Bounty

Basingstoke and North Hants Cricket Club

Basingstoke Cricket Club, an old-established club dating back to 1865, had built up a considerable reputation for the quality of its cricket over its first hundred years. In the early years the opposition was mostly drawn from the surrounding villages and country houses, one of which - Hackwood - had a stronger side and a better fixture list, for example playing against the Free Foresters and MCC in 1888. Gradually the standard of Basingstoke cricket improved - with the addition of county players such as Fred Bacon, Harry Baldwin and Maurice Read - and in 1901 the club was broadened to encompass 'North Hants'. By the First World War Oxford Authentics were among the regular visitors to the picturesque May's Bounty ground and there was an annual two-day match with Eton Ramblers. The fixture list was further developed between the wars to include Surrey sides like Guildford, East Molesey, and Weybridge, while Hampshire Hogs and the Hampshire Club and Ground - defeated in successive matches in the thirties - were frequent visitors.

For the post-war side the stiffest opposition was provided by Reading, with their Berkshire county players, closely followed by Guildford and then the Southampton club sides the Trojans, Old Tauntonians, Southampton Touring Club, and Deanery who, with their base at the

County ground, invariably fielded Hampshire Second X1 players in their line-up. Bernard considers that the Basingstoke team he first joined in 1947 - he was selected on a regular basis from 1951 - was one of the strongest of his time, just eclipsed perhaps by the team which won two consecutive Thames Valley League championships in 1988 and 1989, meeting the rather different demands of the era of competitive league and cup cricket. The sides of the late sixties and the early eighties, in Bernard's estimation, also run these teams very close.

B&NHCC in the late 1940s

When Bernard made up the numbers in that match in August 1947 the team was captained by Howard Lawson who had played for Hampshire as a fast-medium bowler in the 1930s but had completely 'lost' his bowling after the war and was now playing mainly as a batsman. The leading batsmen were Fred Butler - he made four centuries that season - and Guy Daly from Stratfield Turgis who had played one first-class match for Glamorgan before the war. Arthur Wills was a familiar figure behind the stumps, nearing the end of his career, rated by Bernard as the best purely club-level wicket-keeper that he has ever seen, who stood up even to sharp opening bowlers like Bob Smith and Tommy Ratcliffe.

But the star of the side was Guy Jewell, a truly exceptional club cricketer who was a major influence on Bernard's development as a player. To quote the club history, *"Not only is he statistically the most successful Basingstoke bowler, he held many positions for the club......He was at various times secretary, captain, organiser of the Knockout competition, builder of the tea hut, fence repairer, concrete layer, painter, pavilion*

cleaner, barman, taker of 100 wickets in a season, maker of a thousand runs in a season, fete organiser and committee man." (*Basingstoke and North Hants Cricket Club, 1865-1965*, Bichard and Harrison 1966).

Guy Jewell bowled slow left-arm chinamen mixed with occasional orthodox deliveries and he achieved such prodigious turn that it was impossible to position close fielders in front of the wicket. His career (1933-1965) return of 1,820 wickets at ten runs apiece is

GUY JEWELL - Exceptional Club Cricketer and an early influence on Bernard's development as a cricketer

testimony to the confusion he caused to club batsmen. He

performed the Double twice, in 1948 and 1949, in the latter season scoring 1,215 runs and taking 160 wickets. In 1956 he took 166 wickets at 7.11 each and although Jim Laker took all ten Australian wickets twice that season, Jewell went one better, taking all eleven wickets in a twelve-a-side match against the Middlesex player Ian Bedford's X11. This is a feat only performed four times in the history of cricket.

He played regularly for the Hampshire Second X1 during the school holidays but his teaching career restricted his first-class appearances to just one, against Glamorgan in 1951. He also played for Berkshire and the Club Cricket Conference. That he was a true amateur playing for the love of the game is betrayed by the advice he gave to young Bernard to "get out as soon as you reach fifty to give the others a bat".

Bernard as a sixteen year-old on holiday from boarding school, however, extended his first fifty to a score of 67 not out in a win over Hungerford in Cricket Week 1951, while fourteen year-old Clive bowled 28 overs in taking his first five wicket haul (5-77) with off-spin. Clive recalls that his debut for Basingstoke 2nd X1 had been rather less auspicious - run out for 0 with Bernard trying to pinch the strike. It was a source of great pride for Bernard when in the same season he put on a century partnership with his father Reg against N. and S. of the Thames, making 60 to father's 44. The following season he guested for STOATS on tour, scoring 88 not out against Harborne in Birmingham where he faced two future county bowlers Ossie Wheatley (Glamorgan) and Bryan Lobb (mainly Somerset). Still at school, he managed eighteen appearances for Basingstoke in 1952 and twenty-one in 1953, averaging 22 and 29 respectively, when he also represented England Schools and Worcestershire 2nd X1. But from there he fitted in matches for B&NHCC only when other commitments - including National Service, Hampshire CCC and his various football clubs - allowed, although at times it was more convenient to play for Andover where he was living. It was 1966 before he was to be available to play more regularly for Basingstoke once more.

B&NHCC in the late 1960s

Bernard returned to play for the club in Cricket Week in the middle of the 1966 season and ended it topping the batting, averaging 60, while Clive was in second place as well as leading the bowling averages. Captain Mike Bovill in his annual report bemoaned the fact that the brothers were not available more regularly. He had his wish the following season and was able to report that "Bernard scored 1,537 polished runs at an average of 51.23 to give the side a solid background few opponents could equal". Indeed Bernard topped the batting averages for the next decade and more, falling to second place only to accommodate his brother once and his former Hampshire team-mate Bryan Timms twice.

Bernard had strengthened what was already another good side, worthy of the Basingstoke tradition as there were few if any stronger teams in the area. Phil Bichard and Maurice Smith who had both joined the club in the early fifties, now formed a fine opening pair. Both were good enough to play a few matches for Hampshire 2nd X1, the former in the Minor Counties Championship over the 1949-51 period. Bichard was a gritty player, a good worker of the ball with a top score of 184 not out and a healthy career average of over 35. He was also a very good cover field. During one season he had a problem in regularly falling lbw, so he began very ostentatiously to take guard outside leg stump to discourage the umpire's overactive digit - but without any real change of luck. On the tour to Kent in 1967 he had a very painful brush with the pacey Kent county left-armer John Dye when he was bowling for Ashford - but he cherished the bruise on his stomach for weeks afterwards.

Clive Harrison tells the following story: *" I only repeat it because Phil tells it against himself. Phil was a good games player and he became fed up with Bernard rattling on about how good he was at table tennis and all the players he had beaten, so he challenged him to a match. Bernard accepted the bet but Phil was very meticulous and wanted to prepare properly. He bought a table and practised intensively against his son. Time elapsed and it was three years before the match actually took place. When it did Bernard won - but only bothered to play left-handed!"*

Phil's opening partner Maurice Smith was technically very correct and a good-looking player particularly on the off side. He bowled slow left-arm and late on in his career he famously numbered Gordon Greenidge among his victims when he played against Basingstoke for Deanery (.....the hand that caught and bowled Gordon Greenidge).

Mike Bovill, who had played for Dorset, and Bill Ives made up a very good opening attack - Bovill very economical, moving the ball both ways, and Ives in Bernard's words "club cricket's Derek Shackleton, he hardly ever bowled a bad ball and, benefiting from a high arm action, he hit the seam". With Dave Norman as first change with his left-arm over and Paul Harmsworth - who had a season with Hampshire 2nd X1- to bowl off spin, the Harrison brothers often complained that they couldn't get a bowl!

Notable players who made appearances against Basingstoke in the late 1960s included future Test Match players Bob Willis and New Zealander Geoff Howarth who played for Cobham in their early days with Surrey.

Bernard Harrison's X1 at May's Bounty in 1964

The finger of decision

Umpire Peter Collop lifts a finger as bowler Harrison and keeper Griffin appeal, and out goes Reading opener Bampton, lbw, for 35.

(photo: Basingstoke Gazette)

A New Era : The Thames Valley League

Bernard took on the captaincy in 1970 and mostly batted down the order, concentrating more on his swing bowling. The club had enlarged the geographical area - and thereby improved the quality - of its fixture list, and played - and often beat - most of London's top sides like Ealing and Epsom. While for the first time it was able to call on fourteen players with Minor Counties experience, the call was not heeded often enough for the new captain's liking. But the following season produced one of the club's best ever records as the Thames Valley League proved more appealing to the top players and they finished champions in the competition's inaugural season.

To the remaining nucleus of the 1960s side had been added, most significantly, Bryan Timms who batted and kept wicket brilliantly and Derek Dicker whose positive left-handed batting at No. 5 was crucial to the team's first league success. Mike Richardson was an important new recruit - the "best dot ball bowler I ever played with " is Bernard's verdict. He also regularly took a hundred wickets a season at cheap cost. Graham Yallop, the future Australian Test player who was included in Dave Norman's X1 against Basingstoke, struggled to get him off the square. Afterwards he said he was surprised Richardson was not playing first-class cricket. As it was he just played one season for Berkshire.

Back row Peter Collop (umpire), Ron Crossman, Brian Ferkins, Bill Ives , Paul Nicklin, Geoff Passingham , Derek Dicker, Sue Dicker
Front row Phil Bichard, Maurice Smith, Bernard Harrison, Arthur Martin, Clive Harrison, Bryan Timms.

**BASINGSTOKE & NHCC - THAMES VALLEY LEAGUE
CHAMPIONS 1972**

1973 brought a 'brush' with another of the 'greats' as Viv Richards - never to play at May's Bounty in first-class cricket - made an appearance there for Dave Norman's X1 while he was qualifying for Somerset. Bernard tells this story against himself because Richards snicked his outswinger a few times early on - often to the boundary - and Bernard informed all that would listen that he was "just a slogger and unlikely to make it far at the top level". Once Richards found the middle of his bat the ball was often deposited with considerable power into Castle Field as he went on to score 94.

There was a need for younger blood in Basingstoke's ranks and Bernard as captain and coach presided over a decade in which the club nurtured a group of very talented young players who were to serve the club so well, among them Dave Hacker, Danny Bent, Rob Mason, Rob Williams, Richard Keeble and Matthew and Simon Poland. A number of these players were to play for Hampshire Under 19s or Hampshire 2nd X1 but Hacker was the pick of the crop, by common consent for a period of five years the best club batsman around, a right-hander brilliant in the 'V'. He played many fine innings including more than twenty centuries, mostly in the cup competitions, most memorably perhaps a magnificent 90 against John Lever - formerly of Essex and England - playing for Ilford. He had spells with Hampshire and Worcester 2nd X1s, with a top score of 150 for Hampshire. A fine all-round sportsman, he was vice-captain of the GB hockey team at the Sydney Olympics.

BASINGSTOKE & NHCC - 1981
Back Row: Peter Collop (umpire), Mark Cox, Danny Bent, David Hacker, Jim Dixon, Mike Richardson, Matthew Poland, Adrian Godfrey (scorer).
Front Row: Paul Harmsworth, Derek Dicker, Bernard Harrison, Clive Harrison, Steve Rayner.

By the time Bernard handed over the captaincy to Derek Dicker in 1982 the club had started to reap the benefit of the May's Bounty 'nursery' as the youngsters came through the ranks. An important addition was the talented all-rounder Ray Pavesi - to Bernard " the best all-round club cricketer I ever played with" - who in 1991 was to become the fourth player in the club's history, after Bert Butler, Guy Jewell, and Bernard Harrison, to do the Double. Also the batting was strengthened by the arrival of Neil Hames, captain of Buckinghamshire when they won the Minor Counties Championship, and Ian Maynard, a left-handed batsman of considerable flair who played a dozen games or so for Hampshire 2nds. It had been a long wait since the Thames Valley League win - a wait finally ended by a second victory in 1985 -, although B&NHCC finished runners-up on no less than five occasions, were beaten finalists twice in the Bertie Joel Cup - a competition they were at last to win in 1992 - and reached the last eight of the National Cup four times. In cup games the Harrison brothers - both aged over fifty - often opened the bowling in tandem, inevitably now at reduced pace but very difficult to get away. They had really mastered the arts, Bernie's outers and Clive's inners. Bernard had a theory that Clive was more effective up the hill at May's Bounty even though the prevailing wind did not favour his inswing!

The team perhaps reached its peak in 1988, winning the Thames Valley League at a canter and retaining the trophy the following year. Two young players progressed to play for the County - the gifted and aggressive left-handed batsman Julien Wood and Darren Flint, the best slow left-arm spinner since Jewell. Other key players included the all-rounders 'Cardinal' Hume and the hard-hitting Jimmy Govett, Keith Harris, the club's fastest bowler for twenty years who was to take over the captaincy in 1992, and Nigel Williamson, who inherited the gloves from Bryan Timms and also played some forceful knocks.

Fifty and Definitely Not Out

In 1989 Bernard still played in 17 games but he flirted with the idea of retiring - yet, in the words of the *Hampshire Chronicle,* he was to make "more comebacks than Frank Sinatra". He also had Bert Butler's seven decades record in his sights!

Billed as Bernard's final match - 1989
An arch of willow by Old Tauntonians (left) Derek Tulk, Paul Kerley, Fred Miller and others and (right) Stuart Tulk and others.

B&NHCC, one of the few clubs to have maintained the tradition of 'Cricket Weeks', in 1997's Cricket Week honoured Bernard's amazing achievement of fifty years playing for the club. He had clear and fond memories of his first Cricket Week back in 1947.

FIFTY YEARS WITH BASINGSTOKE & NHCC
Cricket Week at May's Bounty 1997

Touring

Reg Harrison had arranged the club's first tour, to the West Country just after the war, and there has been a regular tour schedule since the 1960s. Touring has always been about having fun and socialising as well as playing serious cricket and Bernard - the veteran of 40 such tours - is in his element. He has found his noted skills on the spoons and in juggling to be in as much demand as his cricket abilities. Paul Winn who, with his brother Colin went on a number of tours, remembers one such occasion: *"The Basingstoke cricket team gate-crashed a private party in the hotel and someone introduced Bernie as the world's greatest player of the spoons. He soon had 200 disco-revellers cheering as he played up the men's arms and down the ladies legs!"*

As the organiser of many tours to the Worcester area his skills as a diplomat have also been severely tested when high jinks at various hostelries - if not quite in the rock band class - have got out of hand. Paul Harmsworth was usually the ringleader behind various pranks which often involved him risking life and limb shinning up flagpoles and led to the mysterious disappearance of hotel signs and flags.

While the tradition of touring has been maintained, over the years it has become increasingly difficult to get the best players to go on tour and the cricket has slipped down the agenda, crowded out by competing interests such as golf, booze, and 'pulling' in other than the cricket sense!

Bernard is amused to recall the time when Keith Barker - former Farleigh School pupil and now Basingstoke cricketer - missed his lift and had to travel by train, an uncomfortable journey hiding in the toilet since he was bereft of funds! On arriving at the hotel he drunk his way through all the available optics without apparent effect, but it is not clear who was paying. Dedicated socialising in the bar for some - as well as early morning golf for others - tends to relegate the cricket to afternoon matches only.

However in the early years in particular there was some tough cricket, for example playing Lancashire League clubs on a northern trip in 1971 and Birmingham Municipal regularly on the Worcester tour. The Kent tour in 1968 took in matches against Dover, Folkestone, Ashford and Hastings. The match against Dover at the County Ground is recalled by David Gahan, a teaching colleague of Bernard's who also played some cricket for Basingstoke: *"We were set a considerable target to win, with poor light and the possibility of rain adding urgency. Bernard was the mainstay and he was positively dawdling. In the pavilion we were furious because we felt he was throwing the chance of a win away. But Bernard seemed unconcerned and unleashed an assault in the last two overs, including a 4 and a 6 off the last two balls to win the match. We had, not for the first time, underestimated the little man. Did he ever doubt in his mind whether he could do it? If he did you would never have guessed."*

The sheet anchor is often a key player in a run chase if he can pace his innings, especially if, like Bernard, he is a brilliant mathematician!

The happiest times on the Worcestershire tour were in no small part due to the old fashioned hospitality of Maude and June Holland when they ran the Abbey Manor Hotel at Evesham, a fascinating old building which had been a wartime hospital and was now a hotel much patronised by

WITH JOE AND NORAH MERCER at the Abbey Manor Hotel

famous sporting personalities. One room had a dozen beds in it. According to Ian Crossley Bernard usually arranged for everyone to arrive by a certain time, then made sure he was there first to get the best room for himself. The young lads in the party hardly slept - they were drinking all night, then snatched an hour's sleep before coming down for a generous breakfast served around an enormous banqueting table.

John Adams is a real character on the club cricket circuit and is currently President of Weybridge Cricket Club. He recalls one of the Worcestershire tours in the mid 1970s:

"I vividly remember one particular game captained by Bernie Harrison when Basingstoke played Worcester City in a limited overs match and on this occasion Basingstoke batted first and scored a respectable 220.

At the end of the tea interval Bernie gave me instruction to go straight to the dressing room and put on 6 long sleeved sweaters. Having done this of course as we walked out for the start of the Worcester innings I was elected to bowl and after each delivery I peeled off sweater by sweater. At the end of the over their umpire was covered in sweaters dressed like a Christmas tree, and I was immediately rested. This was not enough to amuse Mr Harrison, as in the final over I was brought back on to bowl.

128

This time I was given the instruction to peel off a piece of clothing after each delivery. Obeying the Captain, after my first delivery I took off my shirt, second delivery my vest, third delivery my boots, fourth delivery my socks, fifth delivery my trousers. With just one ball to go I was wearing just a jockstrap, and can you imagine my amazement when the umpire no-balled me! The last delivery was the Full Monty! I have personally known Bernie for over 27 years and his love for sport and good times is second to none".

The trips to Guernsey started in the late 1970s were also much enjoyed, with hospitality initially provided by Noel Selfe at his fine house and later by David and Julie Nussbaumer who run a magnificent group of hotels including the Cobo Bay. Warren Barrett, the best cricketer on the Island, an all-rounder and fine off-spin bowler, ensured there was some testing cricket too. In recent years there have been trips to Barbados, playing top sides like Carlton when perhaps the touring squad was not at strong as the club would have liked. A meeting with Sir Garfield Sobers was particularly memorable.

With the Great Man - from left to right Paul Harmsworth, Sir Gary Sobers, Bernard, Den Charles and Alan Beresford

There are no longer touring teams regularly visiting Basingstoke - in the past a notable feature of the calender. Over the years visitors have included the Pakistan Eaglets (twice) the West Indian Wanderers (twice), Australian Country X1s, and Lancashire League teams such as Cleethorpes and Oxton.

Inter-League representative matches

Bernard played regularly for the Thames Valley League representative side which since 1979 had competed in the Truman C. C. C. Inter-League. He was captain for three years and he was often joined in the side by other Basingstoke players like Hames and Matthew Poland. Once when he was short of a player in 1982 a phone call to County HQ elicited a useful young player as a stand-in - Robin Smith who top-scored with 17 in a meagre total of 70 against the South African Wanderers. Cardigan Connor while he was with Slough and, most interestingly, the future Australian Test batsman Greg Ritchie who played for Hounslow also made a few appearances for the TV League side. Greg Ritchie also played twice against Basingstoke for Hounslow and for R. Smith's X1. On the latter occasion he was looking for batting practice, but Bernard had not read the script and had him caught behind first ball!

Barbados - a home from home

130

CHAPTER EIGHT

SCHOOLMASTER AND COACH

Bernard's sporting life has been so full that it seems scarcely possible that he also fitted in a long teaching career. In many ways, although his father was a headmaster, brother Clive a history teacher, and sister Grace a dancing instructor, he was an unlikely schoolmaster. His father Reg had earmarked him from an early age for a career in professional sport, while he wanted Clive to go to Oxford University. It is unusual for such fatherly prescience to be so accurately borne out, although he feels that in the end Bernard did not make the most of his sporting gifts. He thought so little of his elder son's academic potential that he allowed his schooling to be sacrificed on the altar of sporting achievement and Bernard left school with just one 'A' level in Pure Mathematics. It did not seem important at the time but in fact he had undoubted strengths in mathematics.

It is ironic, then, that he was to spend around thirty years in the teaching profession and that this phase of his career was ultimately to provide the greatest fulfilment of his professional life. Not that sport was not to figure large in that second career too. It was his sporting contacts who brought the job offers and his all-round sporting skills which made him priceless to the prep schools who were to employ him. The first of these opportunities was at Northcliffe, a very small school just outside Southampton, and resulted from a call from the school to the County ground in search of a cricket coach. He worked part-time and took all games, but he was less comfortable with Geography and History. He came across the inevitable bright spark in the history class who was ahead of him in the text book and kept pointing out Bernard's errors. The new teacher's response was somewhat unconventional - from then he allowed the boy to take the lessons with the satisfactory result that all the class managed to pass their Common Entrance! But, like one of his cricket mentors Guy Jewell, he made up for a lack of academic qualifications with a natural flair for teaching and he kept the children's interest because he had a story for every occasion. Northcliffe provided useful experience and when he left he was succeeded by his county cricket team-mate Mike Barnard.

Philip Watts joined Bernard's next school, Farleigh, as Deputy Head in 1985 and he confirms that Bernard had a real flair for teaching *"preparing topics as he walked through the door. He would go off at a tangent as the mood took him. The children's main objective was to get him to tell one of his many sporting stories for as long as possible. They would often get a good ten minutes worth. But his Common Entrance and Scholarship results were outstanding."*

Through the recommendation of Gerald Williams, the tennis commentator currently with Sky TV and a friend since Crystal Palace days, he had first had a very attractive offer from Millfield School to take Maths up to 'O' level and to coach soccer and badminton. He had turned this down in favour of the Portals job which was nearer home before eventually taking up teaching full-time at Farleigh House.

Farleigh House was a Catholic preparatory boarding school founded by Jocelyn Trappes-Lomax in 1953 and was based in the grounds of the ancestral seat of the Earls of Portsmouth at Middle Wallop, a few miles from Basingstoke. When the lease expired some thirty years later, the new Lord Portsmouth was to reclaim it as a residence and the school - renamed Farleigh School - was to move to occupy a fine house with attractive grounds at Redrice, Abbotts Ann near Andover.

Back in the sixties Bernard was very much thrown in the deep end as Form Master to Form 3, an impressive group of 9 year-olds who included in their number Rupert Everett, future actor of some renown - and friend of Madonna - and Johnny Dumfies, later a Formula One racing driver and now Marquis of Bute. Initially teaching History and Geography once more, in 1967 he was lucky enough to move to more familiar territory, taking charge of all Maths up to Scholarship level. But his first challenge was to face a school inspection, an experience which persuaded him of the advisability of taking a Maths degree. This he did at King Alfred's College, Winchester where he was quite chuffed at the age of 37 to get into the First X1s at football and cricket and to captain table tennis and badminton.

Returning to Farleigh in 1972, he found many changes, including a new status for the school - now a Charitable Trust - and a new Headmaster, Charles Johnstone. The Chairman of the Governors was John Poland, a cricket fanatic whose two sons under Bernard's initial guidance were to develop to play cricket at County 2nd X1 level. In turn John Poland treated Bernard almost like another son. From there Bernard had a most rewarding career, happy days over twenty-eight years presiding over the early development of many fine young games players in cricket, soccer and rugby. Richard Keeble went on to represent England schools at cricket against India. The cricket teams have reached 19 Hampshire Cup Finals and have won 9. William Chignell captained Charterhouse. Indeed many of the cricketers have progressed to perform well in public schools cricket - over 50 appearing in Wisden in that period -, most recently Peter Gretton who scored a century in his first match for Ampleforth in 2001 and over six hundred runs in the season, following James Tussaud's success as an all-rounder the year before. The four Bruce brothers all progressed to play at various levels for Hampshire. James opened the bowling for Durham University in the 2001 season and once for the school took five wickets in five balls - all clean bowled. Alex and Edward are scoring plenty of runs at Eton, while Robert has represented Southern Universities. Two who went on to play first-class cricket were Jack Hamilton-Dalrymple at Oxford University - he also played rugby and is now a priest - and Jonathan Perry at Cambridge University.

Bernard has coached cricket with success over many years - at Hampshire CCC, Basingstoke & NHCC, and Farleigh. He has run courses with Bob Stephenson, Derek Shackleton, Mark Nicholas and Gordon Greenidge. He has a good eye for talent and for correcting faulty technique. Peter Haslop says *"He's a tremendous coach, he's so good at getting things through to the players, and not making it sound complicated, that's what good coaching is all about. He knows a player when he sees one"*.

Bernard is the ideal coach of games. He distinguishes between 'games players' and 'players of games' and places himself very much in the former category. He has always been fiercely competitive - he had to win at everything. His success at games has been based not only on natural ability but on careful study of winning strategies and on the application of mathematical principles whether logic in chess and contract bridge or knowledge of angles in football and cricket. Deputy Head Philip Watts - whose father HE Watts played cricket as an amateur for Somerset after the war - agrees that Bernard was an outstanding coach, instantly spotting where the child was going wrong, *"but what really impressed me was his ability to motivate children. The first X1 results in cricket, soccer and rugby were amazing."*

The soccer at Farleigh has been scarcely less successful than the cricket with many outstanding footballers coming through including two who went on to captain Eton, and six tournament victories at the Douai five-a-sides, while the most recent Rugby 'product' of the school to hit the headlines was Hugh Vyvyan who has gone on to play for Newcastle.

Classical leg-break bowling action: James Tussaud

Celebrity Cricket at Farleigh - 1983

One notable triumph for John Poland and Bernard - among other instigators like Mike Chignell, Alex Holmes, and John Newbury - was the successful Celebrity Cricket match between Colin Cowdrey's X1 and an All England X1 shortly after the move to Redrice. The report in the *Farleigh Review* makes interesting reading.

THE CELEBRITY CRICKET MATCH

Colin Cowdrey's XII v All England XII
on Sunday, 8th May, 1983

COLIN COWDREY'S XII		ALL ENGLAND XII	
D. G. Ufton b Snow	0	R. Swetman c Harrison b Clark	24
J. M. Rice c Parfitt b Murray	67	P. H. Parfitt c Hooker b Durden-Smith	30
N. Durden-Smith b Maru	8	J. R. Gray c Harrison b Durden-Smith	8
M. C. Cowdrey b Maru	0	D. W. Richardson c Woodcock b Clark	1
E. A. Clark c Maru b Wheatley	36	R. Maru c Clark b Lewis	1
R. V. Lewis c Parfitt b Murray	16	P. E. Richardson b Clark	8
R. W. Hooker b Murray	12	K. Wheatley st Stephenson b Durden-Smith	51
R. G. Woodcock not out	1	J. T. Murray not out	10
B. R. S. Harrison did not bat		J. A. Snow c Rice b Clark	4
G. R. Stephenson did not bat		R. W. Merry c Hooker b Clark	0
D. W. White did not bat		F. J. Titmus not out	3
J. S. E. Price did not bat		A. Castell did not bat	
Extras	2	Extras	2
	---		---
Total (for 7 wkts)	142	Total (for 9 wkts)	142
	---		---

Farleigh's cricket season began on this lovely field with a match between two teams of distinguished County and England cricketers. How fortunate are the boys at Farleigh, to play their cricket in such beautiful surroundings and how fortunate to have as Chairman of Governors, John Poland, a cricket devotee and largely responsible for arranging this match; and also to have Bernard Harrison to coach the correct techniques and organise our cricket at Farleigh, with Bill Hicks, as groundsman, who, single-handed, creates good wickets and miraculously tends all our playing fields and gardens.

The game gave many visitors the opportunity to see and admire the grounds of Farleigh, by way of the long curved drive to the school, glimpsing between massive beech trees, the cricket field surrounded by oaks, chestnuts, firs and many other trees.

Unfortunately the weather was always threatening to be unkind, but apart from one stoppage for rain, the game was played to an exciting finish. Previous rain had made the wicket very soft and slow and this, together with the passing years, prevented former England fast bowlers Price and Snow from bowling at their once accustomed frightening, fast speed. The older batsmen found timing on this slow wicket difficult and good hitting came from the younger former Hampshire batsmen Rice and Wheatley. Cowdrey, himself, was bowled for 0, having played his shot minutes before the ball arrived. E. A. Clark had a successful match hitting 36 and taking 5 wickets for 27, but the 'Man of the Match' award went to John Rice for his batting. When the last ball was to be delivered, former Middlesex and England cricketers, Titmus and Murray, were batting and two runs were needed to give All England a victory; but only one run was scored and so the scores were level and Colin Cowdrey's XII were victorious, because of losing fewer wickets.

Farleigh would also like to thank members of Red Rice Squash Club, for their help, Sid Rowles for constructing the score box, Major Chignell, Mr. J. Vail, Mr. Chojecki and all those other Governors and parents who gave their time, energy and valuable assistance to make the day successful and memorable.

Colin Cowdrey's article on cricket all-rounders in the *Country Life* magazine of June 2, 1983, contains many pleasing references to Farleigh School. This was his second visit to this school and Farleigh is grateful to him and to all the cricketers who played in this match and especially the many who had to travel long distances.

COLIN COWDREY'S X1

Back row Fred Houldsworth (umpire), David Matthews, Bernard Harrison, Roy Woodcock, Derek Ufton, John Rice, John Poland, Bob Stephenson, Richard Lewis, Lloyd Budd (umpire)
Front row David White, John Price, Colin Cowdrey, Bob Hooker, Ted Clark
Note the abundance of footballer-cricketers: Ufton, Stephenson, Hooker and Harrison.

FARLEIGH SCHOOL HAMPSHIRE CUP WINNERS 1994
At the COUNTY GROUND SOUTHAMPTON
(Front) - J Douglas, B Grandy, T March, C Norton, J Tussaud, N Louth, G Davies, P Edwards.
(back) - M Emerson, R Horsfall, M Wight. P Plunkett. With Bernard and Richard Keeble.

136

Bernard retired from Farleigh in 1997 and enjoyed a trip to Barbados and a cruise to Venezuela as leaving gifts along with a new set of golf clubs and a Sky TV subscription for life. He is very grateful for such generosity. He lives with his partner Pauline and of course sport still plays a big role in a contented retirement. He keeps in touch with developments via Sky and his continuing contacts at Hampshire CCC, makes optimum use of his golf clubs and pursues his interest in cricket statistics which in the past has seen him contribute to a number of publications including the Hampshire CCC Handbook.

With Cardinal Hulme

Bernard's Retirement Presentation at Farleigh

Since Bernard's retirement Farleigh's sport has continued to prosper thanks to the coaching of Huw Powell, Justin Lynham, and John and Philip Watts, and it is probably the number one sporting preparatory school in the area, winning many trophies at all sports.

APPENDICES

BERNARD HARRISON - STATISTICAL SUMMARY

FOOTBALL

By League	**Appearances**	**Goals scored**
Football League	113	16
Football Combination	80	12
Midweek League	4	1
Southern Floodlit Cup	3	-
Southern League	17	4
Western League	56	16
FA Cup proper	9	-
FA Cup prelim	1	-
Dorset Combination	15	8
Dorset Senior Cup	1	-
Hampshire League (Portsmouth 'A' only)	8	2
Floodlit Friendlies - Crystal Palace	16	6
RAF cup and league Matches	84	108

By Club

	Appearances	**Goals scored**
Portsmouth (all teams)	20	7
Crystal Palace (all teams)	165	26
Southampton (all teams)	33	3
Exeter City (all teams)	46	9
Poole Town	41	12
Dorchester Town	30	11
Andover	1	-
Winchester City	8	2
Portals Athletic	88	52
Lowestoft Town	1	1

CRICKET
Batting

	Mat	Inn	NO	Runs	HS	100	50	Ave
ALL CRICKET								
	2280	1938	561	53556	153*	39	335	38.89
HAMPSHIRE -ALL								
	236	308	46	10116	135*	16	62	38.61
HAMPSHIRE -FIRST X1								
	16	28	2	557	110	1	2	21.42
HAMPSHIRE - SECOND X1								
	101	176	16	5444	135*	8	31	34.03
HAMPSHIRE - CLUB AND GROUND								
	119	104	28	4115	120*	7	29	54.14
WORCESTERSHIRE -ALL								
	4	6	1	148	62	-	1	29.61
BASINGSTOKE & NORTH HANTS								
	1246	917	348	22533	126*	7	41	39.60
ANDOVER								
	38	38	12	1513	127*	2	8	63.04
PORTALS								
	161	149	52	6187	153*	11	42	63.75
THAMES VALLEY LEAGUE								
	16	14	9	205	34*	-	-	41.00
BASINGSTOKE OVER THE AGE OF 40								
	747	481	214	10399	106*	4	54	38.95
AT MAY'S BOUNTY GROUND								
	791	589	235	15931	126	7	103	45.10

Bowling

	Overs	Mdns	Runs	Wkts	5wkts	Catches	Balls/wkt	Ave
ALL CRICKET								
			51888	3031	128	579		17.12
HAMPSHIRE - ALL								
	1265.1	297	3686	121	2	88	63	30.46
HAMPSHIRE - FIRST X1								
	18	4	65	1	-	10		65.00
HAMPSHIRE - SECOND X1								
	787.1	174	2339	62	1	39		37.72
HAMPSHIRE CLUB AND GROUND								
	460	119	1282	58	1	39		22.10
WORCESTERSHIRE - ALL								
	7	0	25	1	-	1	42	25.00
BASINGSTOKE AND NORTH HANTS								
	10561.3	2744	31533	1614	58	319	39	19.54
ANDOVER								
	316.5	50	1012	77	5	6	25	13.14
PORTALS								
	1603.1	347	4439	335	19	44	29	13.25
THAMES VALLEY LEAGUE								
	77	20	227	13	-	1	36	17.46
BASINGSTOKE OVER THE AGE OF 40								
	6363	1682	19347	1002	38	150	38	19.31
AT MAY'S BOUNTY GROUND								
			19824	1011	37			19.61

'THE COMPLETE SPORTSMAN'

YOUNGSTERS TO WATCH

THE COMPLETE SPORTSMAN!

MOST schoolboys play two or three different games, but I have never met one who shone at so many as did Bernard Harrison, the Crystal Palace outside-right.

While at Peter Symonds (Winchester) School, Bernard represented the school at football, cricket, badminton, squash, fives, tennis, hockey, table tennis and athletics! He won the championship at 100 yards, 440 yards, one mile and at cross-country, and was elected Victor Ludorum — champion athlete of the school, and won England honours at

cricket and football, and the Worcestershire junior badminton championship!

Bernard was born at Worcester on September 28, 1934, and moved to Hampshire when very young. Even after leaving school he continued to be outstanding at all games, but decided to concentrate on football and cricket.

Crystal Palace can thank their goalkeeper Ray Potter for Harrison joining the club. The two did their National Service together in the R.A.F., and when League clubs began to get interested in Harrison, Potter persuaded his pal to have a trial with Crystal Palace.

* * *

NO SECOND LOOK

Manager Cyril Spiers did not need a second look before deciding to sign him. He joined December, 1955, and the next April made his League debut.

Crystal Palace, although near

the danger line for the Fourth Division, are far from being down in the dumps. Mr. Spiers has been building a fine side, and in another year should start reaping the benefit of his hard work.

Although there have been no lack of offers for Harrison, Aston Villa being one of many interested clubs, the answer has always been the same: "Sorry, I'm not selling", a reply which also satisfied Bernard, for he is very happy there.

A feature of his play is speed, and he is seldom caught once he is away with the ball, and he makes a speciality of cutting in and shooting on the run.

Harrison was selected for the Southern Section against the Northern Section this year, which he told me was his greatest thrill in football to date.

* * *

Bernard's cricket has developed

as well as his soccer, and he is on the Hampshire County Cricket staff, and is as promising a cricketer as he is a footballer.

His brother Clive is also a fine sportsman, captaining Oxford University at Badminton, and has also played for Hampshire at cricket.

When I asked Bernard who has helped him most in sport, he had no hesitation in replying, "My father, he was always keen on sport and encouraged me in every way."

When the revival of Crystal Palace comes about, I am certain Bernard Harrison will be one of the most talked about wingers in the game; already Southern Section spectators know him as a very fine player.

Maurice Weedon

CRICKET - Hampshire CCC County Championship Winners 1961: 2nd X1 Championship 1967: England grammar schools 1952 and 1953: in club cricket Basingstoke & NHCC Thames Valley League winners 1972 and 1985: RAF AOC cup winners 1954.

FOOTBALL - Football League Division Three: representative side of the old Third Division South 1957-58: England grammar schools 1952 and 1953: Southampton FC League Division 3 winners 1959-60: Poole Town Southern League Division One winners 1961-62: Western League cup winners 1960-61: Horsham St Faith finalists in RAF Cup 1954-55.

BADMINTON - Worcestershire junior champion 1952: all England schoolboys semi-finalist in doubles and last eight of the singles: later a County player for Hampshire: undefeated doubles partnership with brother Clive playing for Basingstoke.

TABLE TENNIS - Andover champion 1967 and 1969: Basingstoke Seniors winner 1975-81: Hampshire Senior colours: with Clive Hacker and Gerald Harvey for Portals winner of Basingstoke and Andover Leagues: many other trophies and medals.

SQUASH - Peter Symonds School champion: Old Boys' Champion 1963 and 1977:Basingstoke Sports Centre finalist 1972 and 1973.

ATHLETICS - Winner of Victor Ludorum at Peter Symonds: cross country champion 1951-53, 100 metres 1952 and 1953, but cricket priorities prevented higher level selection: invited to compete at White City after national newspaper campaign to find the fastest footballer.

HOCKEY - School first X1: invited to play for Hampshire, but football took precedence.

GOLF - Plays off fourteen handicap and has won many prizes.

'THE GREATS'

No book on football or cricket is complete without some lists and the following represent Bernard Harrison's views on the best players drawn from his 'brushes with the greats':

CRICKET

Best played against:	Best seen since the war:
Barry Richards	Barry Richards
Gordon Greenidge	Sir Len Hutton
Viv Richards	Sir Donald Bradman
John Edrich	Viv Richards
Colin Cowdrey	Brian Lara
Alan Knott wk	Sir Gary Sobers
Mike Proctor	Alan Knott wk
Peter Pollock	Sir Richard Hadlee
Frank Tyson	Malcolm Marshall
Bob Willis	Shane Warne
Derek Underwood	Derek Underwood

FOOTBALL

Best played against:
Ron Springett; Bill Ellerington , Bobby Moore, Jim Langley; Frank McClintock, Duncan Edwards, Johnny Haynes, Sir Bobby Charlton; Terry Paine, Geoff Hurst, Cliff Jones.

Best played with:
Ron Springett; Phil Gunter, Len Choules, Alex Wilson; Dick Conner, Cliff Huxford; Terry Paine, George O'Brien, Johnny Byrne, Derek Reeves, John Sydenham.

Not in the GREATS category, but in **CLUB CRICKET** the best Basingstoke and North Hants teams:

Over the seven decades (1940s to 2000s):	The 'Competition Era' (squad based on statistics)
Dave Hacker	Dave Hacker
Ian Maynard	Ian Maynard
Phil Bichard/Lee Nurse	Neil Hames
Julien Wood/Derek Dicker	Julien Wood
Bernard Harrison	Bernard Harrison
Bryan Timms wk	Ray Pavesi
Ray Pavesi	Clive Harrison
Clive Harrison	Bryan Timms wk
Guy Jewell	Jim Govett
Mike Richardson	Charl Willoughby
Paul Harmsworth/Darren Flint	Darren Flint
	Mike Richardson

SELECT BIBLIOGRAPHY

Cricket

Altham, H; Arlott, J; Eagar, E D R; Webber, R (1957) *The Official History of Hampshire County Cricket Club*

Basingstoke and North Hants Cricket Club (1990) *A Celebration of 125 years at May's Bounty 1865-1990*

Basingstoke and North Hants Cricket Club - Annual Reports

The Cricketer

Hampshire County Cricket Club - Handbooks and Scorecards

Harrison, B R S and Bichard, P M (1966) *Basingstoke and North Hants Cricket Club 1865-1965*

Matthews, D (1998) *On the Spot, Derek Shackleton* A Biography

Playfair Cricket Monthly and Cricket Annuals

Wynne-Thomas, P (1989) *The History of Hampshire County Cricket Club*

Football

Bull, D (1998) *DELL DIAMOND* Ted Bates's first 60 seasons with The Saints

Chalk, G and Holley, D (1987) *SAINTS* - a Complete Record 1885-1987

Chalk, G and Holley, D (1992) *The Alphabet of the Saints*

Crystal Palace Football and Athletic Club - Club Programmes and Year Books

Dorchester Town Football Club - Club Programmes

Dykes, G; Golesworthy, M; Wilson, A (1990) *Exeter City* - A Complete Record 1904-1990

Exeter City Football Club - Club Programmes

Fabian, A H and Green, G (eds.) *Association Football* (4 vols. 1961)

The Football Association - Year Books

Neason, M; Cooper, M; Robinson, D (1984) *POMPEY The History of Portsmouth Football Club*

Poole Town Football Club - Club Programmes

Preskett, R (1969) *The Crystal Palace Story*

Purkiss, M with the Rev. Sands, M (1990) *Crystal Palace* - A Complete Record 1905-1989

Southampton Football Club - Club Programmes

General

The Croydon Advertiser

Jenkinson, N (1994) *The History of Peter Symonds School*

The Hampshire Chronicle

Hants and Berks Gazette and Basingstoke Gazette

Peter Symonds School *The Symondian* (School magazine)

The Southampton Echo